I0406912

What Every Son Should Know About Love, Marriage & Divorce:

How to Avoid Heartbreak and Financial Disaster

By

Aaron Burleson M.D.

Aaron Burleson M.D.

Copyright © 2011 Aaron Burleson M.D.

All rights reserved.

ISBN:1461086221
ISBN-13: 978-1461086222
Revision 3

DEDICATION

This book is dedicated to the husbands and fathers who have had their rights usurped, their fortunes confiscated, their labor co-opted and their lives ruined by divorce. Victims of a corrupt system that is more interested in profit taking at the expense of the innocent than in justice or prevention of human suffering. May their father forgive those who have so transgressed even though they know damn well what they do.

CONTENTS

Forward

Men in general are at a disadvantage when it comes to love, marriage and divorce. This is more out of ignorance than stupidity. This disadvantage is even more marked for the man who is or who will become successful financially. Stephen Baskerville PhD in his book "Taken Into Custody." takes a hard look into the divorce industry and family courts describing how they regularly strip fathers of their rights, property and sometimes even their freedom. Since nobody seems to be able to reform this system, the wise man will learn ways to protect himself from it and the disturbed or predatory females it manipulates for it's own gain.

Think of this book as the fatherly advice you should have gotten from your dad and surely would have if someone had told him.

If you are a professional man, or if you are otherwise financially successful, you are in a unique position in our society. Your hard work and dedication have placed you in a position both to benefit society as a whole and to derive for yourself a happy, comfortable and rewarding life. Your intelligence, ambition and work ethic have placed you in a position, which is at the same time enviable and vulnerable.

By the time you have completed your education and training and your career is well on it's way, you will likely be in your late 20's to early 30's, a time in life when many successful men begin to consider fulfillment of the American Dream of a home and a happy family. Your earning power places you in an elite group, particularly attractive as a mate to the deserving and undeserving alike. In some ways your financial status is like a target painted on your butt to those whose intent it is to gain from you by guile and cunning what they were unwilling or unable to gain for themselves through effort and education.

After finishing my residency I looked to the creation of a family but even though my father was an attorney, I had almost no idea of the implications of getting married. A sad fact I lived to regret after only 8 years of marriage. This book is written to help young men make better and more informed decisions about love, marriage and divorce. The knowledge and experience herein, gained over a lifetime, (sometimes at great cost to me personally) can help you minimize the risk of an unhappy outcome in the love and marriage in your life.

I can remember when I told one of my professors that I was getting married, he said **"Don't do that, kid, just find some snarly bitch that you can't stand and buy her a house...you'll be better off in the long run!"**

I was horrified by his sarcasm and apparent cynicism. I chalked it up to an unhappy marriage ending in bitter divorce. What I didn't realize was the marriage I was embarking on statistically had a 50-50 chance of ending up in that very same boat, and further I had no earthly idea of the far reaching consequences that would entail. I know what you are thinking…"There must be some way to better the odds." Read on and discover at least some steps to be taken to improve your chances of success and to mitigate the damage should you fail.

Some readers may feel the upcoming pages contain advice, which could be viewed by some as overly calloused or cynical. If so, they may even continue to think this right up until the time they see their loving bride converted in milliseconds to a heartless predatory bitch by a divorce attorney. It would be great if the whole world was willing to "play nice" but you would be naive to believe this is the case, particularly when it comes to divorce. Remember the old adage "All's fair in love and war"? Well divorce is both, an institution you would be well advised to stay clear of less you become a casualty thereof.

Hippocrates said, " A drastic disease requires drastic treatment." Here's hoping that by facing facts, however unsavory or unpleasant you will be able to avoid the "drastic disease" of divorce in the first place. And if not, at least you can limit the emotional and financial collateral damage.

Throughout the pages ahead I will give examples to illustrate, in most cases, what not to do and to show how unintended consequences, ignorance, or neglect can negatively impact your home life, your marriage, your family and your life as a whole.

To this end there will be "This could happen to you!" sections. These are real-life horrors that can happen to real people. All of these caveats amount to my opinion as I see it or my interpretation of experiences imparted to me by others. Sometimes reading between the lines was required to figure out what actually happened. The names and circumstances are purely fictitious. I intend these sections only as lessons to the reader and any similarities to events or persons living or dead are purely coincidental. Read the sections carefully for they are demonstrative of what can happen if proper precautions are not taken.

Since objective evidence is a much better basis to make an informed decision, there will be suggestions in some sections as to how objective evidence may be gathered. These suggestions are designed to give you a way to determine the truth by collecting objective or experimental evidence using the technological advances of the information age. In some cases there may not be any other way to objectively ascertain the truth. Some of the methods suggested may seem harsh or even underhanded or unethical. Rest assured they will seem mild compared to what you can be subjected to during a divorce, remember an ounce of prevention is worth a pound of cure.

"A second marriage is the triumph of hope over experience." ~Anonymous

If you have experienced the heartbreak of a divorce then you realize the truth of this. Careful applications of the principles discussed here will improve the probability of marrying someone you can stay married to. Also lessen the probability of entering into a relationship with a disturbed or predatory female whose goal it is to take from you the products of your labor.

Chapter 1

The Biology of Love and Mating

"Understanding the laws of nature does not mean we are immune to their operations."
~David Gerrold

My Hypothesis: All human sexual behavior is governed and can be explained by the internal instincts of the individual to either include or exclude certain genetic materiel from the human gene pool.

Internal instincts: Genetically transmitted subconscious behavior patterns in response to a certain stimulus, which are involuntary.

Human gene pool: The sum total of human genetic materiel in living humans, which can be transmitted to progeny.

It is easy to forget that humans are a mere 200,000 years advanced from the Cro-Magnon hunter-gatherers of the past. While our society and our world have changed drastically in this time, at least genetically, we as humans have not. This is simply not enough time for natural selection or evolution to change us significantly. Consequently, we are all walking around with the genetic materiel of those of our ancestors who were successful in getting their genetic materiel into the gene pool, and in having their offspring survive. Contained in this genetic materiel is a set of instincts, which served our forefathers and mothers well in accomplishing this end. An EPROM chip, if you will, containing instructions for behaviors which will insure the survival of the species, pass on high quality genetic materiel and perhaps even cause the species to evolve over time. These are things that we do not think about on a daily basis but which exert their effects on us on a mostly (but not entirely) subconscious level. The basic premise of the hypothesis is that behaviors that were successful in getting genetic materiel into the gene pool are passed on to the progeny as instinct and further, human sexual behavior can be explained on this basis. In the following pages we will examine some common human sexual behaviors and try to determine the gene survival strategy behind them starting with the assumption that human sexual behavior has value in survival of the species.

Three kinds of Sexual Behavior

1) Behavior designed to get individual genetic materiel into the gene pool.
2) Behavior designed to exclude the genetic materiel of certain individuals from the gene pool.
3) Behavior designed to insure the survival of progeny.

Human Mating: The Male Prospective

In the big picture of things sperm is not in short supply in the human environment. An ejaculation contains an average of 300 million spermatozoa but may contain as many as 1 billion. Conservatively assuming two ejaculations a week and an average 40-year reproductive lifespan a single male can produce 1.24 Trillion sperm in a lifetime. Multiply that by approximately 3.4 billion males alive today and that's a lot of sperm.

The challenge for the individual male is to get his sperm into the gene pool and there are two basic strategies for doing this.
Based on primate research male behavior is classified as either Alpha or Beta. Alphas are the strongest and most aggressive males and often have multiple mates. Betas are often smaller, smarter (depending on their wits rather than strength to survive), and usually pick a single mate. There is a lot more to the Beta, which will be covered in detail later.

The Alpha Male Strategy

The alpha strategy is simple, spread the sperm far and wide, find a suitable female, incapacitate or kill any competitors, chase her down, inseminate her and let the cards fall where they may. Once the strategy is completed the Alpha is off to the next female, to the Alpha it is the chase that drives the strategy. The Alpha chooses the female he is interested in based on physical signs of health and child bearing potential. Among those are facial symmetry, which indicates a general good state of physical and genetic health and a waist to hip ratio of exactly 2:3 indicating childbearing potential. However many alphas are not terribly choosey particularly when willing females are available and presenting themselves for mating. This process will be explained more fully in the female prospective.

Looking at the males we know in our lives, it's pretty easy to pick out the Alphas. They may be married legally, intellectually or even emotionally but sexually they are promiscuous and will take great risks to spread the sperm far and wide. The best examples of this that can be sighted are the sex scandals with politicians at their center. Bill Clinton, Elliot Spitzer and John Edwards are just a few examples of this. Considering what these men had to loose, it would seem that their intellect would prevent their indiscretions, but apparently this is often not the case. Such is the power of the instinct to procreate, if you doubted that this instinct was present or doubted it's power, consideration of this single phenomenon should cause you to reconsider. I call it the little head rule.

The Little Head Rule: Alphas often think with the little head because the instinct to get their genes into the gene pool supersedes rational thinking as to the consequences. If this sounds like you and you are unable or unwilling to control your animal instinct, marriage is probably not the best course of action for you.

At best your life will be one of serial polygamy punctuated by bitter and expensive divorces. The unfaithful husband or even one who appears to be unfaithful is the lawful prey of the divorce industry, which will end up with the biggest share of the fruits of your labor during the marriage and even before and after. In marriage thinking with the little head is imprudent, unwise and inherently expensive as will be shown later.

Beta Male Strategy

The Beta male has a two-pronged strategy for getting his genes in the gene pool:
1) Be there to help
2) Be there when the time is right.

The beta chooses one female and tries to gain her favor by providing food, helping to care for the offspring and thus increasing the chances of survival of any offspring they may have together. He will usually be more selective in choosing his one female because there will be only one. His mate may also end up mating with an Alpha, which he will not be able to stop. However the Beta is smart enough to know the Alpha will be off to the next female soon enough and being around more or less continuously gives him an advantage in knowing what part of the ovulatory cycle his mate is in and will probably have a better chance of inseminating her when she is fertile, perhaps repeatedly with successive cycles.

Like the Alphas, the Betas are not hard to identify in modern society. If they are not married they are looking for a wife. The Beta is the boy next door who marries his high school girlfriend (despite the fact that she is pregnant by the captain of the football team). The Beta is the consummate caregiver that provides for and protects his family, sometimes at great personal sacrifice. The Beta will often sacrifice self-interest for the good of the family or offspring. The explanation for this is that the beta has an instinct for the survival of the offspring because it is part of his strategy for getting his genes into the gene pool. This behavior may also benefit the Alphas at least to some extent. Even today the incidence of married couples having children where the husband is not the father is as high as 10% of all pregnancies in wedlock. Most of the time the husband doesn't even know he's not the father.

The Female Prospective

Eggs, unlike sperm, are a much more valuable quantity biologically. Unlike the male who can produce trillions of sperm in a lifetime, egg production of the female is probably about one to two hundred eggs of which perhaps 40 will be viable. In addition, in order to get her genes into the gene pool the egg must gestate, and the offspring must survive until sexual maturity.

The female has two objectives in her strategy to get her genes into the gene pool:

1) She wants the best genetic materiel she can find for fertilization.
2) She can increase the chances of survival of the offspring if the male she chooses hangs around to help provide food, defend the family and help raise the babies until they are sexually mature and self sufficient.

The best genetic materiel will come from the strongest and smartest males; hence the selection process differs considerably for the female. The strongest males will probably be Alphas but an Alpha will seldom fulfill the second requirement of hanging around. In primate societies the females will mate with the Alphas even if they are paired with a Beta most of the time while the Beta will only have coitus with his mate. In this way the female hedges her bets. In order to be competitive the Beta must be smart, a smarter mate will be able to find more food, be more successful in defending the family and also provide genetic materiel that will produce smarter offspring making them more likely to survive. The female often hedges her bets and mates with both Alphas (possibly multiple Alphas) and one Beta. By having sex with the Beta, she keeps him around to help. The female will be more competitive over her Beta than any Alpha she meets because a good Beta is hard to replace while there will always be fresh Alphas sniffing around. Because of this, other unattached females usually will not have sex with a Beta that is spoken for lest she arouse the ire of his mate who may respond aggressively upsetting the social order.

Since the female is the primary caregiver for the offspring, her role is more important in the outcome. In primate societies the standing of the offspring in the social system is solely dependent on the standing of the mother and unrelated to the standing of the father. Perhaps this is because the true father is often not known with any surety. This principle does not hold true in modern human relations because of marriage, making the father's standing more important.

A female whose biological clock is ticking, or even running out can become more seductive towards a male who appears to her to have acceptable or desirable genetic materiel. Among the factors that are considered are size, muscle mass, facial symmetry and intelligence. Perceived willingness to hang around to help raise the offspring is also a definite plus. In primate societies females present and undulate their buttocks to males they wish to mate with. This behavior fits like a key in a lock with the instinctive behavior pre programmed in the male to incite sexual arousal. It is this instinct that is used by exotic dancers in gentlemen's clubs to separate unsuspecting males from their cash. Some of these women have elevated this behavior to an art form. Since humans are the only species that makes love face to face, it is understandable that having structures on the ventral surface of the female that could simulate giggling buttocks would be advantageous. This explains the pure obsession with breasts, cleavage and the like that we see in our modern society. It is because these sexual organs incite instinctive sexual behaviors in men, causing them to think with the little head. It is even used in marketing, and we see it every single day of our lives on television.

In summary, female sexual instinct is governed by three primary factors, in order of importance:
1) Appearance (i.e. strength, health and virility)
2) Perceived ability to support, provide, enable and defend
3) Intelligence.

Sensitivity to emotional issues may also be a factor in the modern world but because of the strong instinct involved in the other factors, this issue is less important. A female may have a strong emotional and intellectual desire to find a sensitive male but upon finding one few females really know what to do with him because their intellect is overshadowed by their instincts. It's the female equivalent of thinking with the little head. The primary factor is getting the genes into the gene pool and for that sensitivity is relatively unimportant.

This could happen to you!

Ben and Lila had been dating seriously for two years and were beginning to talk about marriage. As a surprise for Lila, Bill secured tickets to a rock concert for her favorite band. The tickets were first-class and included a table right in front of the stage. Lila was a beautiful buxom blonde and on the night of the concert she wore a very revealing short dress sporting a lot of cleavage. As the roadies were preparing for the concert Lila and Ben were surprised when one of the band members came up to the table and introduced himself and sat down next to Lila. They were barely 1 min. into conversation when the band member put his hand under Lila's dress. Already drinking, Lila smiled and opened her thighs to allow him full access. In the poor light and mesmerized by the celebrity Ben was unaware of what was going on under the table. Barely 2 min. into the conversation the band member excused himself to return to his duties backstage.

In about 5 min. one of the roadies came up to the table and asked Lila if she'd like to see what was going on backstage. Lila was thrilled and excited and asked if Ben could come along. The roadie said maybe later but there had to be careful about getting too many people backstage right now.

On arriving backstage Lila found the band member waiting for her. Without a word he pushed her into a corner where she sat on a tall stool. Within seconds Lila found herself on the stool, breasts exposed, skirt up to her waist having intercourse with the band member without a condom almost in plain view of numerous support personnel readying the stage for the concert. Lila found it strange that no one paid much attention to what was going on. After he was done with her he gave her an autographed album and send her back to her seat with Ben.

After the concert when Lila and Ben returned to the hotel room Lila was highly aroused and the couple had the best sex of their lives. Two months later Ben and Lila were married and nine months later had a son. Lila never told Ben anything about what happened backstage and to this day does not know who fathered the baby.

The story demonstrates how under the right circumstances a female may instinctively mate with a male, particularly an Alpha, without any thought as to the consequences or expectations of any future relationship. It is obvious that Lila was in the ovulatory part of her cycle. After she was mated she returned to her Beta, Ben. Ben will probably never know that he may be razing the son of a rock star. Ben is not entirely blameless because he failed to defend his ovulating mate from intruder sperm.

Timing Is Everything

"The key to getting the answer you want is the proper timing of the question." ~ *J.R. Ewing*

In the female, the reproductive life cycle is considerably shorter than that of the male. Normally first menses will occur at an average age of 12.5 years and cease sometime in the middle to late 40's. Males on the other hand can still father children well into their 90's.
For this reason, females naturally mature faster than

males both physically and psychologically. They are also endowed with an instinctive reproductive biological clock, which governs their behavior. This is particularly obvious in childless females in their late 20's. In my opinion the perfect age for a female's first marriage is age 28 and first pregnancy age 30. Few males, particularly professional ones, are truly prepared to marry before age 35 making the ideal age difference at least 7 years.

In the U.S. the median age for first marriage is 24.8 for females and 27.3 for males, which means most couples are probably getting married too early.

Males marrying for the first time before age 35 are twice as likely to end up divorced for a number of reasons.

First if they marry women their own age by the time both are 40 many females are already looking old while a man in his 40's is just beginning to look mature. After my first divorce I reentered the dating scene at age 42, I was shocked to learn that the average age of females interested in me was 28. This points out a real difference in what attracts the human female. Where physical signs of health and beauty attract primate females, human females are more attracted by power than by physical appearance. In today's society, power is typified by social and professional standing. Along with this comes wealth and knowledge all of which make such a male attractive as a good provider. If you marry a woman your own age, expect that you will become the unsuspecting target of younger, more attractive females once your wife begins to show her age. Since many of these younger females have a rapidly ticking biological clock, expect to be offered sexual favors by at least some of them. The mature male who is able to withstand such an onslaught is the exception rather than the rule. In my opinion, it is better to postpone marriage until you reach maturity at which time it will be easier to let the big head do the thinking. Also, since you are older, by picking a younger female you can at least partially offset the effects of faster aging in females. This, of course, does not mean that you must be celibate while you are growing up. This is a great time to date a lot of different women of all ages, just be sure to keep your sperm to yourself, and not to think with the little head when it comes to love and marriage. More on timing when we get to Chapter 4 -Profile of a Perfect Wife.

We have placed a lot of emphasis on the male being mature so I think we must now digress and explain exactly what that means. Your first relationship with a female was with your mother and in many ways that has shaped the way you think of females but the last thing any man wants to do is marry his mother, because to do so forever assigns him the role of the child. A mature man will never get married because he is unable to take care of himself. The very definition of maturity is being able to take care of all of your needs yourself. That means, of course, being able to support yourself but it also means doing for yourself all of the things one would traditionally expect from a wife. By that I mean cooking, cleaning, washing, repairing your clothes and generally being able to do for yourself all of the things required for a comfortable life. My Mother used to say. "How are you going to take care of a wife if you can't take care of yourself?" Being completely self-sufficient means that you don't really "need" a wife. Never being needy is a sign of maturity. A truly mature man may desire a wife but by virtue of his self-reliance, doesn't really need one. This same principle applies to the female; a really needy one will usually make a great future ex wife.

Attraction

Perhaps one of the most exciting facets of the human experience is the attraction phase of the male-female relationship. Everyone has experienced this in one way or another. About 60% of communication is non-verbal. The human face has some 200 muscles, which can communicate all manner of feelings and emotions without a single word. Read these signs carefully for better communication. Facial expressions mirror the emotion **and** instinct and humans are often capable of reading these messages in each other's faces, particularly if they are compatible genetically and sexually. There are certain visual clues to general health (facial symmetry), strength (muscle mass), fertility (waist to hip ratio of 2:3), and each partner makes an instinct based genetic compatibility assessment. Often this happens outside awareness but is based in instinct and is the product of successful paring throughout human history.

If it happens to you, you would be well advised to believe and explore it unless you are already paired.

As far as the human experience is concerned the mythology of our culture often immortalizes shared human experience in ways that are universal to us all. For instance, in the story of Adam and Eve, it is written that God created woman, his last and most beautiful creation, for the man. God created Eve just for Adam, he created her to be perfectly compatible with him and when God introduced them Adam recognized her immediately. This is myth, which reflects the human experience of being attracted to someone who is genetically compatible.

Another interesting consideration in females has to do with the ovulatory cycle. In a recent study of females participating in one modern mating ritual, a nightclub event where they are likely to encounter potential mates, females were photographed and then questioned about their menstrual cycle. The females were graded based on their appearance with regard to the seductiveness of their dress. Those females in the fertile portion of the cycle wore shorter skirts, sported more cleavage and wore more aggressive makeup almost uniformly. This held true even for married females who were even more likely to behave in an outwardly seductive way.

There's a take home message here: Know your mate's reproductive cycle, day 14 is not the night for her to go out with the girls. Strangely enough, females that spend a lot of time together tend to get their menstrual cycles synchronized making them a pack of raging competitive sluts right around ovulation time. You should always know when your mate is about to ovulate, even if she is taking birth control. If she is one of the some 50% who will eventually be unfaithful, she is more likely by far to do it when she is ovulating.

The Chemistry of Kissing

The hopeless romantics of you will say that kissing is just the first sign of affection and you would be right but it is so much more than that. Primates exhibit rudimentary behavior that resembles kissing but orangutans don't know how to French kiss. French kissing, or kissing which involves the tongue entering your partner's mouth and which involves exchange of saliva is a purely Cro-Magnon phenomenon. It involves the sense of taste and the sense of smell; it is an important exchange of chemical information. In smelling and tasting your partner the information is likely transmitted in part by pheromones and other substances. Your reaction to this experience is mostly instinctive and the information exchanged involves a plethora of compatibility issues. You may remember the song "It's in his kiss" or as the spaghetti sauce commercial, which proclaims "It's in there!" It's definitely in there. Most of the interaction is subconscious. This is why kissing your sister is reported to be so unpleasant. You are most definitely not genetically compatible with your sister, thus the old saying, "It's like kissing your sister." It is a constant of human experience, you know from the first kiss if you are compatible with your prospective mate.

This is even truer when it comes to oral sex, the instinctive survival purpose of which is to collect information as to health, fertility, and recent sexual activity of your prospective mate. Again, most of the perception is subconscious, the results of which are experienced instinctively or emotionally.

The Chemistry of Love

"Men have died and the worms have eaten them but never from love."
~ Shakespeare from   As You Like It

Stages of Love
    (1) Lust
    (2) Attraction
    (3) Attachment

The lust phase of love is driven by the hormones testosterone and estrogen. Most unattached men and women and particularly women whose biological clock is ticking have healthy levels of these hormones.

In the attraction phase the chemical believed to be most responsible is phenylethylamine or PEA. It is PEA that controls the transition from lust to attraction by affecting levels of dopamine, serotonin, and norepinephrine in the brain. These chemicals are neurotransmitter substances and we believe that the PEA affects their release in specific parts of the brain, which causes the sweaty palms, the stuttering, and what some describe as butterflies in the stomach. PEA is similar in its mechanism of action to amphetamines, which also stimulate the release of these chemicals. PEA can be found in small amounts in chocolate and in large enough doses can give an effect similar to being in love.

Just as with amphetamines, PEA can produce a sort of addiction. And long-term exposure to the compound can produce a tolerance (tachyphalyxis) thus requiring more and more of the compound for the same effect.

These compounds are produced in most relationships for 12 to 18 months on the average. Which explains the waning of the emotional high right around 1 year for most couples.

Hopefully by this time the couple will have reached the third stage of love, which is attachment. The chemicals involved in this process are oxytocin, endorphin and vasopressin. Oxytocin is known as the cuddling hormone and is also one of the chemicals responsible for contractions during childbirth, milk expression when breastfeeding and is released by both sexes during orgasm.

Endorphin is a naturally produced substance, which relieves pain, induces euphoria, and stimulates pleasure like its cousin morphine. Unfortunately endorphin also exhibits the phenomenon of tachyphalyxis, requiring larger doses for the same effect over time. Vasopressin, which is also released during orgasm, has receptors along the pleasure pathway, which are believed to create a mate preference based upon the fact that they reinforce monogamous behavior. Vasopressin production is probably at least partially responsible for successful long-term monogamous relationships.

Meeting Prospective Mates

"A fellow will remember a lot of things you wouldn't think he'd remember. You take me. One day, back in 1896, I was crossing over to Jersey on the ferry, and as we pulled out, there was another ferry pulling in, and on it there was a girl waiting to get off. A white dress she had on. She was carrying a white parasol. I only saw her for one second. She didn't see me at all, but I'll bet a month hasn't gone by since that I haven't thought of that girl." ~ *Mr. Bernstein from* **Citizen Kane**

I've been asked a number of times "where's the best place to meet a prospective mate?" The answer is "you will know one when you see one." Your instincts will tell you when you're attracted and throughout the course of any given day you'll probably see several that meet this criteria. The next step is to check that all-important left ring finger to see if she's taken. If not then it's all up to you.

I like to think of this moment like trick-or-treating on Halloween. She looks good and she arouses an instinctive response from you, that's like finding a good house right on your street. If she has no wedding band, then the porch light is on meaning the house is receiving trick-or-treaters. The rest is up to you, but you won't get any candy unless you ring the doorbell and say, "trick-or-treat!" It doesn't hurt to hold out your bag. Even then, of course, you never know what you are going to get.

The moral of the story is that if you see a girl that you're attracted to and you fail to try to start a conversation or get to know her then nothing will *ever* happen. All of this involves some risk but only the risk of being rejected. You need not take this personally, perhaps she doesn't feel the same attraction that you feel but remember nothing ventured, nothing gained. I think the best approach is to start a conversation about anything, the clothes she's wearing, the book she's reading, what she has in her grocery basket or even the weather. Remember to be polite and to introduce yourself after the first couple of sentences. Usually after the introduction things will warm up if she's interested. Be sure to watch her body language carefully if she adjusts or puts her hands through her hair, this is a sign she's interested. After that, the game is afoot and it's up to you to exchange phone numbers or make future meeting arrangements.

Talking on the phone is a wonderful way to get to know someone. There's very little risk and you can find out a lot about a person just by talking on the phone. Since you are not face-to-face the nonverbal portion of the communication is eliminated thus simplifying the interaction. The average person has about 40 hours of conversation in them and most people love talking about themselves. This works just as well for someone that you've met online. 1 of 5 relationships now start online and this may be a good place to start if you're the shy type. Keep in mind that the pictures you see maybe more than five years old and that the person may be more than five years older and weigh 50 pounds more than stated! Fortunately all you have to lose is time and during your phone conversations or e-mails you've gathered the information you need to eliminate those who have obvious red flags. This can be a fairly efficient and inexpensive way to screen candidates without becoming too involved right off the bat. The big advantage to starting a relationship on the phone is that by the time you meet face-to-face you already know each other pretty well and are comfortable talking. I haven't intended this as a how-to book because what works for one person may not work for another but this should be enough information to get started.

Thinking With the Big Head: An Unnatural Act

"God gave us all a penis and a brain, but only enough blood to run one at a time."

~ Robin Williams

OK, you are mature enough, you just met a girl that your instinct tells you is compatible and you think she is soooooo hot. Now you are at a crossroad. Being mature when you reach a crossroad you read the signs. To do this requires overcoming your instincts and thinking with the big head. If you are thinking with the little head you may read all the signs, end up throwing rocks at them and then going the wrong way only later realizing that the crossroad was clearly marked but you, in your haste, lust and primitive emotional state failed to read them correctly. If you must give in to your animal instincts, at least be truthful to yourself about what is transpiring setting a safety point further downstream for the big head to again assume control once some of the lust has been expended but before you are in over your (big) head.

Please do not misunderstand, an instinctive attraction and determination of genetic compatibility as described above is essential to a happy relationship, even a happy life. However, the presence of such a connection does not by any means insure a successful relationship.

A better aid in predicting a successful relationship and avoiding a disappointing one is the reading of the signs present in every relationship and to do this you must be ready willing and able to look for and interpret the signs correctly and objectively, in other words you must engage yourself in an unnatural act - ***thinking with the big head***

Aaron Burleson M.D.

.

Chapter 2

Red Flags

You are Advised Not to Ignore

Remember drivers Ed.? What traffic signs did you have to learn first? The warning signs of course. Ones like "Bridge out" "Dead End" and "Dangerous curve."

We will start with red flags which are easily identified anc the mere presence of which disqualify your potental mate for consideration as a marital partner. We will call these

Red Flags That are Absolute Contraindications for Marriage

Illegal Drugs

"Don't do drugs because if you do drugs you'll go to prison, and drugs are really expensive in prison." ~John Hardwick

Any prior or present use of methamphetamine, cocaine or heroine, particularly if that use was intravenous or involved crack cocaine disqualifies any prospective mate. Amphetamines, cocaine and opiates are all highly addictive and anyone using them at any time in their life will always be at risk of a relapse. If your prospective mate has ever done this, she is disqualified. Period.

Other illegal recreational drugs like marijuana or ecstasy are relative contraindications depending on the duration and frequency of use and must be considered on a case-by-case basis. Experimentation with these substances is fairly common. When looking for red flags, things like dependency, impairment, frequent or continuous use should definitely be considered disqualifying factors.

Any history of trafficking in illegal or controlled substances are also disqualifying unless you fancy visiting your spouse in jail.

Prescription Drugs

"It is easy to get a thousand prescriptions but hard to get one single remedy. "   *~Chinese Proverb*

 Prescription drug abuse and misuse has become a monumental problem in this country. Part of the problem is that we've somehow come to expect that for every problem there's little pill that will fix it. Despite what big pharmaceutical companies would have you to believe, nothing could be further from the truth. Every drug however benign it may seem can have side-effects, interactions, unusual reactions or may have unintended consequences attributable to it's use.

Any kind of continuous prescription drug use should raise a red flag, indicating further investigation is needed to elucidate the factors, which may have occasioned its use. Among the causes may be chronic disease, hypochondriasis, psychiatric conditions, substance abuse, inadequate personality disorder, or any number of other underlying causes or conditions, which may affect the advisability of entering into a long-term relationship.

There is a great free app for all the smart phones called **Epocrates.** This app will identify medications by their appearance, tell you what the drug is for, warnings, contraindications, the drug class, whether it's a controlled substance, it's interactions and how it should be prescribed. This app is for doctors but it can also help you to evaluate drugs your prospective spouse might be taking and also uncover why she may be taking them.

How do you find out what she might be taking? Usually all you have to do is ask. Most of these women have no idea of the implications of their prescription drug use. Some of them even see their condition as a badge of honor and will happily tell you that they have ADHD or that they are bipolar. After you have asked, then take a look in her medicine cabinet or anywhere else these drugs may be kept. If she has lied about what she is taking or left something out, that should be a big red flag. If you suspect that "miss Right" may be taking any of these drugs ask to see her pharmacy records or have her submit to a random drug test. Refusal to provide this information probably means she has something substantial to hide.

Testing Your Prospective Mate for Drugs.

If you are serious about her and there is even a hint of a drug problem, then it's time for some objective testing. You can request a random drug test outright and if she refuses then there's probably a problem.

You can also test your prospective mate for drugs without her even knowing it. This is done by taking advantage of the fact that the first thing girls do when they come home after a night out is to head for the restroom. Prepare the restroom for drug testing by interrupting the water supply to the commode by turning off the supply valve. Then flush the commode until little or no water remains. Remember to put the seat down and unscrew one or more of the bulbs that light the bathroom. You don't want the bathroom to be completely dark but you do not want her to be able to easily see that there's not much water in the toilet either. Be prepared to collect the sample with a turkey baster and sample bottle handy. While she is in there knock on the door to hurry her up telling her that you need to go to the bathroom too. When she finishes she'll find out that the toilet will not flush. Tell her not to worry that you'll take care of it but you have to go the bathroom now. When she's out lock the door and collect the sample. It can now be tested for all the illegal drugs, amphetamines, opiates and pretty much any other class of drug you see fit.   Remember urine testing only measures drugs taken with the last 24 hours or so.

Hair can also be tested for many of the same things and if you leave a brand-new hairbrush in your bathroom for her you should have a good supply. You can also collect small amounts of hair while she's sleeping but this is a little bit more risky. Hair testing is preferred if you wish to detect drugs taken over much longer period of time.

There are many testing laboratories on the Internet and it is suggested that you refer to these sites for procedures before collecting the samples.

This may seem a little bit sneaky to some of you but if you're about to dedicate your life to a women by marrying her you have a right to know what you're getting into. Just be sure you don't share the results with anyone else because some may consider this an invasion of privacy or even slander

Red Flag Prescription Drugs

I advise you to consider the chronic use of any of the following prescription drugs a disqualifying factor for a prospective mate.

(1) Amphetamines such as Adderall
(2) Opiates such as hydrocodone, codeine, etc
(3) Psychotropic Drugs

    a. Antidepressants, particularly those in the selective serotonin reuptake inhibitor (SSRI) class such as Prozac, Celexa, Cymbalta, Paxil, Effexor, Zoloft and many others

    b. Benzodiazepines (Xanax, Valium, Tranexene and many others)

    c. Antipsychotics drugs such as Phenothiazines (Serentil, Melaril, Prolixin and others.)

    d. Lithium
       (Consult the Internet For a more complete listing of drugs in each class)

Amphetamines

This Could Happen to You!

Tom, a general surgeon was married to Belle, an energetic 40-year-old housewife. Since turning 40 she had been spending 2 to 3 hours at the gym each day trying to loose some weight. To help her loose weight Belle convinced her doctor that she had ADD for which she was prescribed Adderall. Shortly after starting the drug Belle became paranoid and began to imagine that Tom was having an affair with one of his assistants at the office. Nothing could have been further from the truth but wherever Belle looked in Tom's life she found things she misinterpreted as proof of Tom's infidelity. As time went on Belle's condition deteriorated and she became delusional. Belle was unable to distinguish paranoid fantasy from reality. The drug also left her unable to sleep at night and she would often awaken Tom at 2:30 am to discuss his cellular phone bill or emails on his computer. It mattered little to Belle that Tom had five cases scheduled for the next morning. There was no reasoning with her, no amount of proof was enough, as Tom soon found out there is no way to prove you are not having an affair. Tom probably would have understood what was happening had he known Belle was taking this drug but unfortunately he and Belle were in the middle of a divorce by the time he found out. If your wife is paranoid and delusional about your fidelity, believe me, you will be getting a divorce. Its possible Belle was a compensated Bipolar. When she started taking the Adderall it exacerbated her insomnia, which led to her paranoid state and delusional fears. The whole thing ended in a bitter divorce. We will pick up on Belle and Tom's story later.

Adderal is really only methamphetamine repackaged. It is marketed in the U.S. as a treatment for Adult Attention Deficit Disorder or ADD. It is a class 2 narcotic, and likely the most addictive prescription drug on the planet.

Most of the people taking this drug don't really have this disorder but are taking it off label for weight control or performance enhancement in school or sports. If this drug is found in the urine of an athlete or racehorse they will be disqualified from competition. It is just as addictive when prescribed as when taken illegally. It can cause worsening of pre-existing psychiatric or personality disorders as well as insomnia, paranoia and psychosis.

Opiates

There are plenty of good clinical reasons to be using this class of drug for pain relief such as a root canal, a broken bone or even a sprained ankle. But one must remember that these drugs are opiates and as such are highly addictive particularly with chronic use. What you're looking for here is a history of chronic use and/or addiction. Signs of this may be a prescription for the same drug from multiple doctors or use over a protracted period of time. The chronic use of methadone may indicate that the person was previously addicted to heroin. In any case use of these drugs over a long period of time may indicate other problems such as an addictive personality. Any person in possession of a large quantity of these drugs should be suspected of selling them on the black market. All of these drugs are controlled substances and there is a reason for that.

Psychotropic Drugs

The use of any psychotropic drugs should at least be considered a relative contraindication for consideration as a potential mate because by their very nature these drugs alter brain chemistry and thus behavior. If your prospective spouse is taking one of them there is no way to know what her real personality is like. If she stops the drug you may be left with whatever is behind door number two. What she may be like after years of chronic use is what is behind door number three.

Antidepressants In the Selective Serotonin Reuptake Inhibitor Class (SSRI's)

"In the 1960s, people took acid to make the world look weird. Now people that think the world is weird take Prozac to make it look normal."
~Unknown

In 2008 worldwide sales of this class of drugs amounted to $10.9 billion dollars. (Hell the whole dam NFL is only a 9 billion dollar market!). So many of these drugs (SSRI's like Prozac) have been prescribed that these drugs can actually be detected in the water supply! Some experts say these drugs are being overprescribed. **Ya Think?**

Although some patients use these drugs for situational depression or anxiety their chronic use usually indicates a serious depression or Axis 1 diagnosis (personality disorder). You will be surprised how many people are taking these drugs chronically. As for SSRI's the F.D.A. labeling says that they should be taken for no longer than 6 months. Gynecologists, Family practice and internal medicine doctors hand this stuff out like candy without any significant psychiatric examination other than a history of depression or difficulty sleeping, and many patients have been on these drugs for years. They are technically not physically addictive but rapid withdrawal can precipitate a psychological crisis. They can certainly be emotionally addictive and many patients have a fear of stopping them. My advice is to pick someone who doesn't need to alter his or her brain chemistry with a happy pill to deal with his or her daily life.

Benzodiazepines

This class of drugs includes drugs such as Valium, Xanax and Tranxene. They are most often used for anxiety and I really don't have a problem with patients using them for short periods of time to control anxiety caused by situations which are temporary such as an out patient surgery, airplane flight, or other situations which may temporarily cause anxiety. These drugs are very much like alcohol and thus can be dangerous if taken together. They are moderately addictive and can cause seizures on withdrawal from someone who is addicted. If used chronically, recreationally or with alcohol these drugs are surely a red flag.

Antipsychotics

 The use of these drugs usually indicates a serious Axis 2 diagnosis such as bipolar disorder or schizophrenia, and is an absolute contraindication for consideration as possible mate. This class of drugs is not widely prescribed and usually not overprescribed. Most of the people taking these drugs are under the care of a psychiatrist for a serious psychiatric problem.

The problem with axis 2 disorders is that they can be relatively stable or compensated for relatively long periods of time when the patient seems relatively normal. This balance may be affected by many factors such as medication, environmental factors and external events. The problem with this is that no one can be in control of all the factors and that the balance may be fairly delicate and thus the line between sanity and psychosis, mania, or depression can be quite thin. For more information read the section below on psychological disorders.

Lithium

 Lithium is an element that when taken internally

interferes with sodium metabolism particularly as it relates to the nerves and the brain. Technically the drug is described as a mood stabilizer. This drug is used almost exclusively for treatment of bipolar disorder or what used to be called manic-depressive disorder. The drug is prescribed to control the manic phase of this disorder when the patient experiences flight of ideas, insomnia, grandiosity and even paranoid or delusional behavior. Bipolar disorder is a serious condition and those suffering from this illness can bounce back and forth between the manic and depressive phases. Some cases can be quite unstable with the smallest external event causing a switch between mania and depression. Some of these patients who are on the manic side of the illness chronically have been described as outgoing, bubbly, energetic, and friendly. As long as they are compensated reasonably well they can get along in society without attracting too much attention. But when they become frankly manic or frankly depressed pretty much everyone in their life suffers. Patients in the manic phase can sometimes go out on a huge extravagant shopping spree maxing out all the credit cards and spending the available balance in the bank accounts. While in the manic phase reasonable and rational behavior is suspended and replaced by grandiose or frankly irrational behavior. While in the depressive phase these patients are particularly prone to commit suicide

Alcohol Abuse

Alcohol is a legal substance, which is used extensively in our society to lubricate the wheels of social interaction. A prospective mate who drinks irresponsibly however can be a problem that is difficult if not impossible to overcome. Notice how your perspective mate conducts herself in the social environment where adult beverages are served. Although most people have at some time in their life been intoxicated, if your prospective mate is making it way of life she probably has an alcohol problem. Since alcohol problems tend to run in families, she may have a family history of alcohol abuse as well. Other signs that alcohol may be a problem are driving while under the influence, missing work due to alcohol consumption, loss of memory for prior events when intoxicated and hoarding or hiding alcoholic beverages or otherwise concealing how much alcohol has been consumed. It usually does not take a rocket scientist to discover if someone has an alcohol problem but only a congenital idiot would ignore such a problem in a prospective mate.

Drug Use Conclusions

Hopefully you have read and understood this section on drugs and alcohol. Sadly this problem may be present in up to 50% of prospective mates who might otherwise be acceptable. A relationship with and particularly a marriage to someone who has a substance abuse problem or who has a psychological, emotional or physical problem, which requires chronic use of drugs to control, presents a **clear and present danger** to love, marriage and a happy life.

Psychological Conditions

Obviously you want your spouse to be mentally healthy and free from personality disorders. Taking on a wife with an axis 1 or axis 2 diagnoses would definitely be ill advised. It's bound to be trouble in the long run, no matter how benign it seems at any one point in time.

Testing Your Mate's Psychological State

If there is any doubt, a professional evaluation may be in order, however you will not be privy to the results without her permission. If you suspect that this is needed and your prospective spouse refuses to cooperate then this is grounds to eliminate her as a potential mate. There is nothing worse than a mate with a psychological problem who is in denial or who refuses to cooperate for diagnosis and treatment.

 One good resource which describes both axis I and axis II disorders is the DSM–IV diagnostic manual. If your prospective mates behavior seems bizarre or you find yourself scratching your head calling into question her judgment perhaps you should curl up by the fire one evening and read the DSM-IV. If the description of one or more of the axis I or axis II disorders has her picture right next to it you may be in trouble.

I have included this link to a psychological diagnosis page; the tools found here will help you decide if there is a real problem based on your observations. Since you are probably not a trained observer you cannot rely on the results as an accurate diagnosis, only as a guide to help you decide if professional intervention is required.

http://www.psyweb.com/Diagnosis/Diagnosis.jsp

The following are some additional red flags that should raise the question of your prospective spouse's mental health.

Self Image

"I would not want to belong to any club that would have me as a member." ~Woody Allen

Any signs of distorted self-image should be taken seriously. For instance an obviously thin girl who constantly talks about being too fat has an altered self-image. This usually comes about from an overly critical parent and any history suggestive of this can be a big problem.

If your prospective mate doesn't love herself your love for her can be a sign to her that there must be something seriously wrong with you!

Anorexia and bulimia are potentially serious psychiatric conditions, which have as their primary cause a distortion of self-image. Persons suffering from these conditions look at themselves in the mirror and see someone who is markedly obese when they're actually dangerously thin. This leads to self-starvation and in the case of bulimia to self-induced vomiting. There is no good treatment for these conditions, which can sometimes be fatal.

Less serious defects and self-image can still be highly disruptive to any long-term relationship. Before anyone can accept your love they must first love and approve of themselves. A sense of inferiority can lead your spouse to jealousy or to seeking approval wherever they can find it. This need for constant approval may lead a person to behaviors that can be highly destructive to themselves and others. Sometimes no matter how much approval is provided it proves to be inadequate to overcome the overwhelming feeling of inferiority. This can lead to resentment and various forms of acting out in the quest to receive approval from someone.

Body Piercings and Skin Art

"I think body piercing can be a good thing; let's you know right off when something ain't quite right about someone."- Hank from King of the Hill

These things are a matter of taste but in my opinion it is a self-image issue. Well-said, Hank.

Family History

It's always a good idea to look carefully at your prospective mates family history. Such things as divorce, mental illness, traumatic events, and all manner of other happenings can affect your relationship going forward.

Divorce affects different people in different ways however children are usually significantly affected particularly if they're between the ages of 6 and 15.

Children in preadolescence or early adolescence are usually affected the most. Many have self-esteem issues, self-image issues or worse. No matter how well adjusted a child of divorce seems to be the politics of their family of origin will follow them throughout their lives shading their decisions, expectations and aspirations. Unless the family was particularly dysfunctional I think it is fair to say that adjustment and socialization will usually be better in a prospective spouse whose parents stayed together. The mere presence of a divorce in your prospective spouses family of origin is not a disqualifying factor. It depends on how she adjusted to the loss and to what degree it has affected her ability to establish and maintain a relationship of her own.

Family Relations

It should be fairly obvious if your prospective spouse comes from a dysfunctional family. Of particular interest is her relationship with her father. Her relationship with him was the model for all other relations with the opposite sex. If she is critical of her father, openly hostile, or continually in conflict with him it's likely to be a problem for you regardless of whether the father or the daughter is primarily responsible for the conflict. It just doesn't matter; any woman who can't get along with her father is going to have the same problem with her husband sooner or later. Show me a girl who loves

and respects her father and I'll show you one that is
capable of love and respect for her husband. Remember
that the converse is also true.

This Could Happen to You!

 *Belle had a stormy history with her father. As the middle
child, Belle was always told that she was supposed to be
a boy. She spent a lot of time with her father growing up
and on vacation usually went with him sharing his
activities while her sisters went with their mom. When
Belle was 13, time for the family vacation came around
and Belles father called her to his study to tell her he
wasn't going on vacation with the family because he had
to work. Belle was devastated. When Belle, her Mom and
her two sisters returned from vacation, Belle's father had
moved out of the house and in with his young mistress. A
bitter divorce ensued and Belle didn't spend any time
with her father for almost 2 years. Although Belle loved
her father very much, she never forgave him for his
betrayal of her and her mother. Further she harbored a
subconscious fear that Tom would eventually betray and
desert her just as her father had so many years ago. Her
fears became delusional under the effects of Adderall.
Belle constantly berated her father and made fun of her
stepmother behind her back, had Tom only realized how
big this problem actually was he could have ditched Belle
when they were dating for a healthier partner. The fuse*

on this power keg smoldered for 9 years before blowing up in Tom's face. Tom ended up paying for the sins of Belle's father because he failed to heed one big red flag. We will pick up on Belle and Tom's story again later. To be continued....

(Damn, Tom, how many red flags did Belle have anyway? Answer: 13)

While you are looking at her family of origin also look at her mother. How her mother treats her father (or current mate) and how they get along generally will be the model she will use to when interacting with you. Also most of her mothering skills will come from her mother so notice how mom treats the kids because your prospective spouse will probably treat your kids the same way, should you have any.

Here is another important tip that I learned from my father. Look at her mother to get an idea how she will age. Over a lifetime I have learned this to be universally true, my sister and all of my female cousins have aged just as their mothers did. This is also true of most of the girls I went to high school with. This was the take home lesson of my 20-year high school reunion. Dad was right when he said women age like their mothers.

Your Prospective Spouse's Role

All families have rivalries, sibling, Oedipal, and other, nobody's perfect. However it behooves you to observe how your prospective spouse interacts, particularly with her immediate family. If she is willing to lie to them, doesn't treat them fairly, steals from them or cheats them in any way you have to ask yourself if she treats her family like that, how is she going to treat you? You would be surprised how many men see this behavior and either ignore it altogether or make excuses for their prospective spouse. Again, only the presence of the behavior is important, it matters not what justification she may have for her actions or who is at fault.

Sexual History

As described above, seeking approval can often take the form of sexual promiscuity. This is principally true of anyone who has a history of sexual abuse, particularly abuse in the pre or parry adolescent stages of development. Many people are willing to talk about the abuse they suffered at the hands of family members and others. Keep in mind that any history of this is a serious red flag because it's so difficult to overcome even with many years of therapy.

This Could Happen to You!

After Bell and her father were separated at age 13 her mother was ill equipped to supervise her activities. According to Belle one of her father's friends who was affectionately called "Uncle Louie" made a rendezvous with her at a fancy hotel. After being plied with alcohol she was taken to an opulent room and there deflowered by her father's friend some 30 years her senior. As distasteful as this is, she liked it. Over the next few years uncle Louie availed himself of her charms intermittently. Everyone was oblivious to this behavior and to the terrible toll this took on Belle and her self-esteem.

When she was 16 one night late after having too much to drink she in was pulled over by two police officers. Belle's reaction was to put on her "fuck me" pumps and screw her way out of this difficult situation. She met the two officers at their apartment and had sex with both of them thus avoiding a DWI and confirming her worthlessness as a person just as her father and his friend had taught her.

Any history of promiscuous behavior especially with multiple partners or at an early age may indicate an abuse or serious self-image problem. This is probably as good a time as any to examine closer the two faces of promiscuity. I will start by asking the rhetorical question, "What is the difference between a slut and a whore?" A slut behaves seductively and bestows sexual favors indiscriminately because she craves the attention it gets her, she may or may not enjoy it, depending mostly on whether she gets the approval she needs. If she does not get the approval she is seeking then this served to prove that her poor self-image is correct and that she is in fact worthless. If the approval is provided it's like a fix of an addictive drug which encourages her to continue to act out in the same fashion. It's a catch 22. The basic problem underlying this condition is the subconscious self-image and is often quite resistant to change even with therapy.

" I never do anything for free."- Ruby the Heart Stealer

A whore on the other hand has come to the conclusion that she is worthless but has learned that others can be manipulated and taken advantage of using her sexual favors. By being paid, this is proof positive that she's worth at least something. She sees herself as unloved and unlovable, by her actions she proves this over and over to herself and others. By profiting monetarily from what she's done, she's able to extract at least some semblance of self worth from the cold cruel world having already closed the door on any possibility of experiencing happiness or self-esteem.

The average number of sexual partners between puberty and age 28 would probably be around 2 to 5 for most females these days. Anything over or under this may represent a problem. Virgins are probably not the best choice because you always run the risk of them developing curiosity about what it would be like to have sex with someone else if they become bored or disillusioned after you're married. Inexperienced or virginal females often have unrealistic expectations regarding love and sex and are sometimes easily disillusioned. Females tend to develop a greater degree of maturity after they become sexually active and for many the experience improves their judgment but a potential partner that's been frankly promiscuous may find it difficult to change these ways after marriage. One must consider any history of promiscuity as a great big red flag.

Bisexuality

"The best thing about being bisexual is that it doubles your chance of finding a date on Friday night."

- Anonymous

This could happen to you!

Larry and Marsha had been married for 10 years. They had three children ages 9, 7 and 5. Larry felt that it was a happy marriage until one day his secretary came in and said," There's a sheriff's deputy here to see you." The deputy identified himself and asked Larry his name then handed him an envelope full of papers, which turned out to be a divorce complaint from Marsha. Included in the papers was a restraining order preventing him from returning home. Larry later found out that his wife's lesbian lover, Terry moved into the house with his wife and their three children that very day. By the time the divorce was over Larry was paying alimony and child support sufficient to support Marcia and her new nontraditional family with not one but two stay-at-home mommies!

I guess I don't understand it myself but a lot of men get very sexually excited when they see two women having lesbian sex. Most bisexual females don't even consider it cheating if their lover's another female. The truth is if your prospective mate is bisexual then that effectively doubles the number of people she can cheat on you with. Further bisexual females are often fickle and unstable subject to the whims and the admonitions of their homosexual partners. This is a big red flag and sooner or later it will mean trouble in River City.

Sexually Transmitted Diseases

Obviously nobody wants to be married to someone who is HIV-positive or infected with hepatitis C. Other sexually transmitted diseases such as gonorrhea can leave a woman unable to conceive. A history of multiple infections, even of treatable sexually transmitted diseases demonstrates poor judgment at best and probably indicates multiple sexual partners.

Jealousy

"The jealous bring down the curse they fear upon their own heads." ~Dorothy Dix

If ever there was a red flag that would cause you to grab your hat and run this is it. Watch carefully for signs of this green-eyed monster for it has the capability of tearing your relationship and your life apart.

Jealousy literally always comes from a self-image problem or insecurity on the part of the one who is jealous. There is nothing anyone else can do to solve this problem. No amount of reassurance, demonstration of affection, or love can have any effect on it whatsoever. It is the sole responsibility of the one who's jealous to resolve this problem. If your prospective spouse is shown signs of jealousy then she must be judged solely on her ability to control it.

If your prospective spouse tries to make you responsible for her jealousy and insists some change in your behavior is necessary in order control it then she is not taking responsibility for her own feelings and you can rest assured this problem will get worse rather than better as the relationship matures.

It is not love that is blind, but jealousy. ~Lawrence Durrell

This Could Happen to You!

Now back to the story of Tom and Belle. From the beginning of their relationship Belle was always extremely jealous, Sometimes insanely so. Whenever they went to a social gathering Tom was always walking on eggshells. Anytime Tom spoke to another woman or even looked at one for more than a moment this sent Belle into a jealous rage. Sometimes she would not speak to him for days at a time after such an event.   Once Belle started her Adderall the problem became much, much worse. Belle became delusional, jealous of everyone Tom worked with. Belle would not listen to reason about any of her feelings.

One day on the way home from the gym Belle passed one of the girls that was employed at the office where Tom worked. Belle ran the frightened girl off the road and confronted her physically screaming at the top of her lungs.

Fortunately for Belle the cops did not become involved, however unfortunately for Tom the girl made a complaint with his employer. Tom was called in and told that if anything like this ever happened again he would be terminated. Now Tom's job itself was at risk subject to Belle's irrational behavior.

Again the price of ignoring a big red flag becomes evident. Tom knew Belle was insanely jealous. He also knew she was insecure due to a self-image problem. She told him about the abuse at the hands of Uncle Louie before they were married. He also suspected that she might be bipolar even before they were married. Any one of these things should have been enough for Tom to realize what he was getting into. Tom loved Belle but no amount of love will overcome these kinds of problems, which will ultimately come to dominate the marriage. Consequently Tom paid a high price for his stupidity and neglect, as the reader will learn in subsequent chapters.

Previous Relationships/Baggage

By the time we are ready to get married I suppose all of us have at least some baggage leftover from previous relationships. If you insist on carrying this baggage, you would be well advised to pack light. If your prospective mate has been married before or in a relationship, which she expected would end in marriage but did not, then her feelings about these relationships, need to be explored carefully. Many times there will be some emotions left over from the relationship, which she applies to men in general. If there are then you can expect that these will be projected upon you sooner or later.

A lot of people think it's bad taste talk about prior relationships however if you're considering a prospective mate I believe it is essential.

Bad Kids

Children from a prior relationship will almost always present a challenge. This is particularly true in the preadolescent and adolescent stages of their lives. Even if they no longer live at home your spouse will always feel an emotional responsibility for them.

Since you are not the biological parent, your authority over and influence on these children will always be limited.

A kid that will lie, cheat and steal will be heartbreak to biological and step parents alike. Most of the child's morality is learned before the age of six and by the time they have reached this age it is difficult to make significant modifications in their approach to life.

One must remember when marrying a spouse with children from a prior relationship that you are also marrying those children as well.

If your perspective mates kids are constantly getting into trouble this speaks to her mothering skills as well as to the aggravation and interruptions they will create in your marriage. If your prospective mate defends her children's indefensible behavior, then you can bet this will be a source of constant conflict in your marriage. They're not going to get rid of the kids if conflict becomes unbearable they'll get rid of you instead.

Treatment of Strangers

Observe carefully how your prospective spouse treats others, particularly those in powerless positions like domestic help, waiters, sales clerks and the like. If you get the idea she thinks she is better than they are or that she treats them disrespectfully she will probably do the same thing to you if you're not getting along or if you become persona non grata as the result of a divorce.

Alternate Realities

" There's a sucker born every minute!" ~ P.T. Barnum

Does your prospective spouse believe in astrology, crystals, fortunetellers, ghosts, aliens from the mother ship, Sasquatch, the Loch Ness monster, or that Lee Harvey Oswald acted alone? If so she may have trouble staying in contact with reality in other areas. There are a number of women out there whose contact with reality in areas such as these is tenuous at best. Sometimes these beliefs and superstitions can be very strongly held, if so your prospective mate can be a target for con artists as well as believers of much of this mumbo-jumbo. Best pick a spouse whose feet are firmly planted on the grounds of reality. Otherwise you may find yourself taking trips to faraway lands looking for an energy vortex or paying $500 to join a séance trying to contact Eleanor Roosevelt. In addition to being incredibly stupid these things can also be incredibly expensive.

Honesty

"Anyone who doesn't take truth seriously in small matters cannot be trusted in large ones either."
- Albert Einstein

Whenever I hire a new housekeeper, on her first day working alone in the house I always leave a $20 bill on the floor in the laundry room. If when I come home the $20 is on the kitchen counter with a note "I found this on the floor in the laundry room." I know the housekeeper can be trusted. If not and the $20 is gone the housekeeper is fired on the spot. Don't you think evaluation of a prospective spouse's honesty is at least as important as hiring a housekeeper?

As you get to know your spouse, you will have many opportunities to observe her behavior as it relates to honesty and ethics. This is not something that can be taught after childhood. Ethics come from one's parents and the learning is by example. It always pays to familiarize yourself with your prospective mate's parents. One poor girl's father said to me "In life there are only two rules:

Rule #1: GET THE MONEY

Rule #2: REFER TO RULE #1."

(He was a lawyer, of course). I sure hope she's happy with her new boyfriend. Enough said, with a father like that you know she never learned one whit about ethics from him.

In the case of honesty it's better not to ask, anyone can talk the talk but do they walk the walk? Notice what your prospective spouse does when she gets too much change back at the grocery. Does she pocket it and walk away gloating later that she just got an extra 5 bucks or does she call the clerk's attention to the error and return her ill gotten gains. Does she cheat on her taxes or on a test at school? Dishonesty by any other name still stinks. If she is willing to sell her integrity for such a low price now just wait and see what she is willing to do in a divorce.

This Could Happen to You!

Frank was a successful investment adviser in his own firm. Lorna was Frank's executive assistant. Lorna was very young and beautiful but she was also married. Frank and Lorna became very attracted to one another as they worked together. Before long they were involved in a hot and heavy extramarital affair. It wasn't long before Lorna's husband found out and filed for divorcee. Before the ink was dry on the divorce Frank and Lorna got married. They bought a nice house together and moved in, all seemed well for the first couple of years. Frank was happy and content with his sexy new wife.

One day all the planets lined up and the three appointments Frank had for the afternoon all cancelled. Frank was elated because he was now going to get to spend the afternoon with his lovely wife Lorna.

When Frank got home he made his way through the kitchen and family room and down the long hall to the master bedroom. As he neared the open door he heard the slurping animal sounds that everyone would recognize coming from the bedroom. That's right the lovely Lorna was getting the high hard one from an old boyfriend right there before Frank's eyes. Frank was caught so completely off guard for a moment he didn't even realize it was Lorna. Frank backed off mortified and crept back down the hall and sat in his favorite chair and tried to think to the sounds of his "lovely" wife having sex with another man in his bed. Frank finally realized that if he stayed any longer or confronted them he would probably take a shotgun to the both of them. Not wanting to spend the rest of his life in prison Frank decided to fight Lorna with his hat, he grabbed it and ran. Frank's Caddy left a half block of screaming rubber in front of the house. Frank drove right through town and off into the countryside. He drove for hours thinking about what had happened. He finally checked in to a hotel and got stinking drunk. This was the last thing he would have ever expected from his beautiful sexy wife Lorna. As it turned out Lorna had a few other surprises left for Frank. When Frank came home the next morning he found that Lorna had gone along with Frank's collection of gold Krugerrands amounting to $22,000. Frank never got them or Lorna back. To add insult to injury in the divorce Lorna got the house.

 This just goes to show how bad things can turn out if you ignore a big red flag. You are out of your mind if you marry someone who cheated on his or her current spouse to start a relationship with you. It seems to me that this happens all the time. Perhaps the people that do this think that there's something different about their relationship that makes it somehow special or at least more special than their lovers relationship with their previous spouse.

Always remember the leopard does not change its spots. *Once an adulteress, always an adulteress.*

Testing your Prospective Mate for Honesty

" Trust but Verify". -Ronald Regan

If you want to know for sure, try a variation on the $20 on the laundry room floor trick. Put at least 100 bucks in an envelope, stamp and address it to your great aunt Maude. The more money you put in envelope the better the test will be. Now while she's not looking, drop the envelope in the parking lot next to the car where she's going to get out. Do this while she's waiting for you to open the door for her and make sure it lands right where she's going to step when she gets out of the car. That should at least make for some interesting conversation over dinner. Either aunt Maude gets a nice surprise in the mail and you keep your prospective spouse or your now ex girlfriend gets a new pairs of jeans for the best 100 bucks you ever spent.

There is no substitute for honesty and integrity, further it's not possible to have a happy marriage without it. If your prospective spouse has shown any tendency to lie, to cheat or to steal, however minor the offense may seem, it is more likely that she will be your future ex-wife rather than your life partner.

Friends and Associates

Another excellent way to assess your prospective spouses suitability as a life partner is to examine her relationships with her friends and associates. As my grandmother used to say, "birds of a feather flock together ". Included in your evaluation should be the same personality traits, drug habits, ethics, intelligence, education, and other factors that you used in evaluating your prospective mate. Further the evaluation should include some assessment of the degree to which her friends can influence your prospective mate's behavior. Also important are the durations of these friendships and the various aspects of your perspective mate's life they include. You must realize that even after marriage your wife will be influenced by her friends, the amount of judgment she shows about this can be the difference between a successful marriage and a divorce. It is also important to evaluate the relationships the friends have with other men, if they're attached how they treat their husband or boyfriend is paramount. If your wife's best friend is involved in a divorce it may not be long until you're involved in one also.

This could happen to you!

Bob and Francis have a marriage that was the envy of all their friends. Francis's best friend Jill has just filed for divorce. During this time it is to be expected that Jill will lean on Francis for support during her time of need. As the divorce progressed Bob found that Francis was spending an inordinate amount of time with Jill. Sometimes Francis would be at Jill's house for the entire evening not coming home until 10 or 11 o'clock at night. At first Bob understood this but after while Francis was spending so much time with Jill this began to irritate Bob. When Bob confronted Francis about this he found that she was quite defensive and mostly unwilling to listen to Bob's concerns. What Bob didn't realize was while Francis was at Jill's a large part of what she was hearing were complaints about Jill's soon to be ex-husband. Unfortunately for Bob, Francis had some of the same complaints about him and hearing Jill talk about it brought to the forefront some resentment towards Bob. As time went on the conflict between Bob and Francis escalated and before the whole thing was over they found themselves in the middle of a divorce as well.

This story points out succinctly just how much a woman's friends can influence her life and yours if you happen to be married to her. Ideally all your wife's friends should all have happy and successful marriages.

Since this will not always be the case it is important that your wife realizes the shortcomings of her friends and how this may affect your marriage. You should be able to assess this even before you're married. With a little attention to your wife's friends and how she reacts to their shortcomings you should be able to assess the degree of influence they have over her and the soundness of her judgment concerning them.

If your prospective spouse is listening more to her friends than she is to you this may be a big red flag. If her friends are critical of you or of men in general it is probable this will adversely affect your relationship. It is important to remember one's choice of friends often reflects the views and attitudes one holds intrinsically. Even though it may not seem so, if your wife is hanging around with a bunch man haters, it is possible that she may be a closet man hater herself. You can save yourself a lot of trouble by eliminating women like this from your life before your wedding day.

Male friends

If your prospective spouse has male friends then there may be a problem. Male friends whom she spends any significant amount of time with will eventually have an adverse effect on the relationship. The more time a male and female spend together the more likely they are to come become romantically or sexually involved unless the relationship is purely professional or work related, even then it can and does happen. Any such relationship should not involve a social component, which is exclusive of the spouses of the persons involved. Once a relationship becomes serious it is unwise to tolerate any significant solo social contact with those of the opposite sex by your prospective mate. On this issue I agree with Dr. Laura and this goes for you as well as for your spouse, close friends of the opposite sex will be nothing but trouble In the long run and should be considered incompatible with a happy marriage.

The Feminist

"Can you imagine a world without men? No crime and lots of happy, fat women." ~Marion Smith

It goes without saying that any woman who is a raging feminist with a chip on her shoulder cannot be expected to perform well in the role of wife. Many of these women are angry man haters and will make you very uncomfortable in the role she has cast for you as chauvinist pig. These feelings are learned behavior and should be considered the same as a prospective mate that cannot get along with her father. (Many times the two conditions co-exist). Unless you were raised in an unconventional family, the feminist will fail to meet your expectations of a wife and mother in the long run.

 In my opinion it is even worse if your prospective mate is only a closet feminist. These young women show up sporting tons of cleavage and wearing a dress so short they need two hairdos, usually right at ovulation time. If you show any reaction whatever then you're accused of treating them like a sex object. In other words they claim for themselves the right to full expression of their instincts while insisting that you strictly control yours. In short they wish to have their cake and eat it too. By that I mean they expect candy on Valentine's Day, they expect you to change the tires and open the doors for them but they're the first to hit you with a big gotcha at the drop of a hat calling you a male chauvinist pig if you behave like anything but a eunuch. If you have any kind of brain in your head or an ounce of self-respect you will grab that hat and run rather than marry one of these women.

PMS Issues

"You know what PMS stands for? Putting up with Men's Shit" ~Anonymous

I've heard some men say it stands for "pass my shotgun"! We've already discussed several good reasons for keeping up with your spouse's menstrual cycle. Well here's another one. By convention the first day of the menstrual cycle is the first day of bleeding. Although individual women's cycles may very the normal cycle runs 28 days. Usually the bleeding subsides in 5 to 7 days. On the 14th day of the cycle ovulation occurs. Premenstrual syndrome or PMS can begin as early as day 17 or as late as day 23 and usually subsides once menstruation begins or shortly thereafter. If your spouse suffers from PMS it may last anywhere from 5 to 11 days. Keeping up with her menstrual cycle will let you know pretty quickly if your prospective spouse suffers from PMS.

The cause is unknown but many believe it to be caused by the effects of hormonal changes on the brain. It is also believed that various social, cultural, biological, and psychological factors may affect it. The symptoms include fatigue, difficult concentration, depression, sleep disorders, forgetfulness, mood swings, poor judgment, poor self-image and irritable, hostile or aggressive behavior including outbursts of anger. The syndrome affects different women differently and the severity of symptoms varies considerably. If your prospective mate suffers from this condition it can obviously have a big effect on the relationship particularly if it's severe.

In my opinion women suffering from significant PMS will have a particularly difficult time with menopause, which usually occurs in the middle to late 40s. This is one of the times when couples tend to get divorced.

 If you constantly find yourself in conflict with your prospective mate during this portion of her menstrual cycle then PMS is probably the cause and you must decide if the relationship can weather 5 to 11 days of this every month. If the symptoms are severe and resistant to treatment or if your prospective mate resists treatment this is a red flag that should not be ignored because the problems will likely become much worse during menopause. Further, this monthly trial by fire will take a toll on your nerves and your marriage.

Abortion

The author has considered long and hard whether to include this section. As a matter of due diligence it must be included even though the issues are complex and convoluted. What follows is purely a matter of opinion and is expressed as the best opinion of the author and submitted for your consideration.

A history of abortion leaves a scar on the heart of the person who undertakes this act. If that person is under 18 and therefore a minor, they should not be burdened with the gravity of this decision at this time in life. The decision to have an abortion before age 18 is the responsibility of the girl's parents. It matters not whether the parents were involved or not. If they were not involved they damn well should have been. Few girls under 18 have the capacity and understanding to make this decision. This being said, decisions about this matter, which occurred before the age of 18 cannot be held against the girl.

I admit that the selection of age 18 is arbitrary but it is also the age of majority according to law. Therefore in order to try to give some guidelines I have chosen this arbitrary age as the age of consent. Few 18-year-olds have half a brain, however this is the age when the law begins to hold them responsible for their actions.

After age 18 an abortion shows poor judgment at best and a callous disregard for human life at worst. In the course of my work I've heard every excuse for a woman having an abortion. The first one is that they didn't trust the father to help care for the children. My response is, "Why did you put yourself in a position to become pregnant by him then?" Following this there are plethora of other excuses for being unwilling to take responsibility for their irresponsible acts. In my opinion an abortion after age 18 shows an unacceptable hardness of heart and a particularly selfish outlook on life. I am not opposed to abortion because I feel I do not have any right to impose my morals upon others. But I do have the right to decide for myself what I think is right or wrong. Further I also have the right to include or exclude others from my life based upon my judgment of their past acts. If they have done things that are purely selfish and would show disregard for the sanctity of human life then they can have no place of trust in my life. In the final analysis each person much look into their own heart and decide how abortion affects them and what they believe concerning this issue. I only offer my own opinion and do not and will not stand in judgment of the beliefs and opinions of others unless it affects my life directly. (Which, of course, it would if I were contemplating marriage.)

Financial Responsibility

"Every woman should have four pets in her life. A mink in her closet, a jaguar in her garage, a tiger in her bed, and a jackass to pay for it all." ~Mae West

The number one cause of strife in a marriage is financial instability. Difficulties with the finances can be particularly hard to solve if either of the persons involved is financially irresponsible. Financial irresponsibility creates resentment, which builds insidiously undermining the very heart of the marriage. Resentment can also be created when one spouse strictly controls the other's spending even if such an action is necessary to prevent an irresponsible spouse from overspending. This points out the importance of picking a spouse that is financially responsible in the first place.

Take a close look at your prospective spouses finances. Does she have more than two credit cards or credit cards that are over the limit? Is she behind in her car payments or rent? Does she buy extravagant things she cannot afford either for herself or for others? Is she able to live within her means or does she rob Peter to pay Paul to make ends meet? Has she ever been denied credit or written a hot check? Can she go out and buy a new car today or would she have to go to "buy here pay here" for those who have no credit? Does she shop at expensive department stores and pay the asking price or does she shop for sales and frequent the bargain or discount retailers? Does her cell phone service or utilities get interrupted for nonpayment?

Does she have deferred dental work that needs to be done? Does she have creditors calling her right around dinnertime?

A spouse with a low credit score can affect your credit score as well. Also if she is heavily in debt you may have to assume or clear this debt when married. This can be like a terribly large millstone around your neck when starting a marriage.

If your prospective spouse is at least the recommended minimum age of 28, is she gainfully employed? What kind of employment history does she have? Has she been in the same job for the last five years or has she had five jobs in the last two?

Financial responsibility is usually learned at home. Look at your prospective spouse's family of origin if they're affluent and she was born with a silver spoon in her mouth she may have expectations as to the standard of living, which is acceptable to her, or spend irresponsibly. If there was always plenty of money when she was growing up she may not be able to understand that her new family cannot afford the things that her parents could. Being used to an inexhaustible supply of money she may take this attitude toward your bank account and become irate when it is exhausted.

If she came from a working family who struggled to make ends meet she is likely to be frugal and a good steward of the family finances.

If she grew up in a family that was fraught with financial problems poor credit, payday loans, being behind in the bills and being irresponsible about finances generally may seem normal to her, just a part of life. In this situation being confronted with a bank account, which is not overdrawn, may be an irresistible temptation to her.

All financial habits can be changed but it's like the old joke about how many psychiatrists does it take to change a light bulb? Only one but it takes a long, long time and the light bulb has to really, really want to change.

It is not unreasonable to ask for credit report and a financial statement from a prospective mate. If you do this be prepared to provide her with your own. What's good for the goose is good for the gander. You can be sure if she's unwilling or unable to provide this for you that there's a problem.

There are ways to deal with a financially irresponsible spouse. Separate bank accounts are probably always a good idea in the beginning to allow you to control strictly how much of your financial resources your spouse has access to until she can prove that she's financially responsible. In this situation, if she has an income, it is important that you make her responsible for at least some of the household expenses, preferably the ones she has control over like her cell phone bill.

Chronic Medical Conditions

I will not speak here to the advisability of entering into marriage with someone who has a chronic medical condition. This is something everyone has to evaluate for himself or herself based on his or her own values. However I should point out that marrying someone with a chronic medical condition will certainly place a financial and emotional strain on the marriage and the implications of this should be considered carefully before proceeding, particularly if the potential mate has not been forthcoming about the condition.

However you may feel, some conditions should constitute an absolute contraindication to marriage. HIV, Hepatitis C, history of venereal disease of any kind are a few of the obvious ones.

Genetic Conditions

There are a number of genetic conditions that can be manifest or recessive genes that can be carried which can be passed on to your offspring. Some of these conditions can be quite serious which is why family medical history is so important in selecting a prospective mate. Most of the time all you have to do is listen when your prospective mate is talking about her family or listen to what her family members tell you when you're at family gatherings. People with chronic medical conditions mostly love to talk about them, which bores most people to death. You'll be surprised at what they tell you if you seem interested.

The Hypochondriac

Beware of the person with multiple signs and symptoms of medical problems with no obvious disease. You may have already identified this tendency in your prospective mate based upon the prescription drugs she is taking. The hypochondriac is insecure and thrives on the secondary gain and attention he or she receives when others think she is ill. These persons also are addicted to the attention they get when they visit their physician. They usually will not be satisfied with the visit unless they come away with some medicine. A person like this can greatly complicate your life and run up a lot of medical bills. It depends of course on the severity of the condition and must be viewed on a case-by-case basis

There is another condition, which is called Munchausen's syndrome. Named after the Baron von Munchausen, persons suffering from this condition are paranoid and delusional about their health and addicted to the attention they receive from healthcare professionals. These patients will feign illness and often have had multiple, often unnecessary, surgeries before the diagnosis is made. This condition must be considered in any case where there's a long medical history or history of multiple surgeries.

Lazy Mary

Here's another really important red flag. Unfortunately, laziness as a condition is incurable. Look for signs of this condition in your prospective mate. Does she put the dirty dishes in the dishwasher or leave them in the sink?

Is she content to sit around the house and watch TV all day? Does she expect you to wait on her when she never waits on you? A lazy wife will sooner or later figure out that after the divorce you will still have to pay her but she will not be required to do anything whatever for you. No, it's not fair so protect yourself from the terminally lazy.

Physical Aggression / Impulse Control

"How do you fight a woman? With your hat, you grab it and run!"   ~Anonymous

If your prospective mate has a problem with aggression or impulse control then you may be in for a rough ride in marriage. Any history of physical aggression, outbursts of anger or impulsive behavior, which is destructive, falls into this category. Examples of this are striking another person, throwing objects or destruction of property. This type of behavior shows a lack of impulse control and can be a hospital offence resulting in injury or death. A history of physical violence towards any other person or anything else indicating a lack of impulse control that includes an obvious disregard for the safety or property of others disqualifies that person as a prospective mate.

Putting Her Best Foot Forward

When evaluating a prospective mate for red flags, one must remember that during the attraction phase, she will be on her best behavior. Anything that is obvious here will more than likely become worse (if not much worse) once you are committed and she is feeling more comfortable and secure in the relationship.

Anything you find from this section must be taken seriously even if it seems insignificant. What you are seeing may only be the tip of the iceberg. It is up to you to investigate potential problems with due diligence.

Chapter 3

Profile of the Future Ex-Wife

"Insanity: doing the same thing over and over again and expecting different results."
 ~Albert Einstein

Before proceeding towards marriage with anyone, one needs to look carefully at all their former failed relationships for in them you will find all the signs and symptoms of the future ex-wife. Remember carefully all the relationships that you had which were a disappointment to you or which ended badly. You'll probably be able to find a lot of similarities among them. It is very important that all your prior failures be categorized and collated carefully to avoid making the same mistakes in the future. Look for the red flags that you obviously missed. If one particular flag occurs in multiple relationships then you need to be particularly careful to look for this in your prospective spouses. And more important is to look for the red flags that you knew damn well were there and decided to ignore. If your prospective mate has one of these things you know you're about to marry your future ex-wife. If you do not understand the failures in your relationship history then you are doomed to repeat them.

Thinking with the Little Head

The sine qua non of a future ex-wife is one that is selected for purely instinctive reasons. Rest assured that if a physical attraction is the only thing you have going for you in a relationship that that relationship will do well to last a year as a marriage. Remember what we learned in chapter 2 about the natural history of love and the physiologic changes incurred at 12-18 months. No matter how sexually compatible you may be in the beginning you must remember that sexuality will be of limited use in solving the problems which will inevitably arise. As you spend more time together you will become desensitized to the sexual aspects of the relationship and if this is not replaced by deeper feelings (which are based more on your intellectual and emotional compatibility) then the relationship is doomed to die of boredom. You have to ask yourself what would you do while you're living "happily ever after"? Rest assured the answer is not sexual.

Are you Listening?

You Have friends, family and associates that know you well. These are trusted sources of objective information and one sure way to marry your future ex-wife is to ignore their warnings.

This is especially true if they know you well. If they know your prospective mate well also then you'll be privy to an invaluable source of information that may save you from a terrible mistake.

If the source of the information is trusted and/or loved you're bound to consider it carefully unless you have insisted on thinking with the little head. Oftentimes people in this kind of position, where they know both people involved can see inconsistencies or red flags that you cannot. To ignore admonitions or warnings from such a person is ill advised, do it at serious peril to your life, your family, and your pocketbook.

The Devil in a Red Dress

"She seemed to mean what she said. She said pretty much this: I retained some lawyers, I have to move on with my life, I am divorcing you, and then she added, I need money. "
~Dennis Kozlowski

Or should I say a dress made of red flags. One red flag should be enough to look elsewhere for your prospective mate. If the only thing she is wearing is a dress made of numerous red flags stitched together then you have a future ex-wife for sure. If you are aware that this is the case and having difficulty taking the appropriate action then go down to the sleazy part of town on Friday night and pick the roughest honky-tonk you can find. (Something like the "Dew Drop Inn") Walk up to the biggest meanest guy in the place and make a few off-color comments about his mother and let Bubba try to beat some sense into you. At least you'll have some time to think about what you're about to do while you're in the hospital.

The civilized thing to do however is invoke the rule of the 50 ways. The rule of 50 ways is based on the old song by Paul Simon "50 Ways to Leave Your Lover".

The chorus goes something like this:

You just slip out the back, Jack.
Make a new plan, Stan.
You don't need to be coy, Roy.
Just get yourself free.
Hop on the bus, Gus.
No need to discuss much.
Just drop off the key, Lee
And get yourself free.

Chapter 4

Profile of the Perfect Prospective Wife

Timing is Everything

Your perfect prospective wife will be single, not divorced or in the middle of a divorce. She should be at least 28 years of age if you are talking about an American girl. She should be at least 7 years younger than you. You need to have known her for a minimum of 2 years and have been in an exclusive relationship for at least one year. It's better if you have cohabitated for at least a year as proof of concept that you can stand each other 24/7 and to see how much of the attraction, if any, wears off after a year. You both need to be finished with your education and training and be gainfully employed. (Yes, both of you). She needs to profess by word and deed that she is ready willing and able to become your wife and that she is willing to wait at least 2 years after you are married before getting pregnant.

Intelligence, Education and Earning power

If you look at physicians who got married during their training or before the divorce rate exceeds the average at 60%. If they get married after their training the chances of being divorced are only 30%. If married to another physician the divorce rate drops to 11%.

The take-home message here is that if you marry someone whose intelligence education and earning power match your own then divorce becomes much more unlikely. On the other hand if the little head is doing your thinking and you marry a trophy wife who has no skills no education and no earning power then your marriage will be like a house built on sand. As her physical assets begin to wane then you have nothing to fall back on. In a healthy relationship sex will only be about 10% of the relationship with the rest being friendship, shared values, shared interests and then a mutual caring, what some would call love. In a healthy relationship the sex is just the reward for getting the rest of the relationship right.

More than anything else that you can do, picking someone who could match your intellect, your education and your earning power greatly reduces the risk of your marriage ending up in a divorce. You still have to pay attention to all the other red flags but a great disparity in intelligence, education and/or earning power should be considered a red flag in its own right. Sure an educated professional woman with earning power can be a little bit more difficult to deal with in the beginning but the rewards of being successful in this kind of relationship greatly outweigh the effort required to establish it.

Similar backgrounds

Certainly spouses with similar backgrounds tend to communicate better, have a better understanding of each other and life in general and more compatible expectations of what it means to be a spouse. This is not to say that spouses that have significant cultural differences cannot work these out but both parties have to be committed and show exceptional patience and understanding. Issues concerning expectations, goals, and the means by which goals are to be achieved must be discussed at length in advance to make sure aspects important to each partner are addressed in detail before these issues result in conflicts.

Religion

If either you or your spouse is religious people then it goes without saying that it's best if you are of the same or at least similar religions. This is even more important if e ther spouse tends to be on the radical side of religious thinking. If you are a fundamentalist Baptist it would be best if you could pick someone who is also a fundamentalist Baptist. Less compatible would be another Protestant such as Methodist or Presbyterian. Less compatible yet would be Roman Catholic. Although still Christian, Catholicism differs greatly from the Protestant religions. Still further would be a Jewish spouse which although western still has very different traditions and expectations. Unacceptable differences arise in the case of Muslims, Hindus, Confucians or other Eastern religions. Again I'm not saying it's impossible to have a successful marriage with someone whose religion is significantly different from yours I'm just saying that it's a lot more difficult, carries with it a lot more risk of divorce and is something that bears a lot of consideration prior to the marriage.

Shared morals, values and goals

You need to spend plenty of time talking about your values and your goals. This includes but is not limited to professional goals, personal goals, family planning and long-range plans for the future. Your perfect prospective wife and you should agree on all these things prior to getting married. You need to be particularly vigilant of the way she answers these questions to be sure she's not just telling you what you want to hear. It should raise a red flag if you're agreeing on everything without much discussion or need for compromise.

Hygiene

It is wise to remember that when you marry someone you will be living in close proximity to him or her pretty much 24/7. Take a close look at your prospective mates hygiene habits as it pertains to herself, her home and her car. The perfect prospective mate cares about her appearance and puts forth the effort to ensure sanitary and orderly living conditions. Even if you're not a clean freak yourself, living with a woman that's a pig at home and too lazy to keep the house clean will wear on you over time. The perfect prospective wife takes pride in her appearance and in her home.

Mothering skills

If your prospective mate has children already this will be an easy evaluation to make. If not it's still not impossible. Look at how she interacts with her younger siblings, if any, or how she reacts to children in general. Look to her family of origin and how her parents related to their children. Strangely enough a look at her pets can sometimes give you a good idea of her mothering skills. This is particularly true of dogs if she raised the dog from a puppy.

Test Your Prospective Mate's Mothering Skills

Here is another test for your prospective mate and this one will actually be fun! In excellent way to test your prospective mates mothering skills is to give her a puppy! A puppy is an excellent child substitute and one that is just weaned and crying for its mother is a really good choice. This test should be begun early because it will take about a year to assess the results. For the test to be valid she has to be the primary caretaker for the dog. As the dog matures her mothering skills are evaluated based upon the dog's behavior. If the dog is obedient, good-natured, people loving and friendly all of these are good signs. If the dog barks at everything, howls all night and craps on the floor, all of these could be signs of trouble. Also notice how she reacts when the dog needs discipline. Does she take on the task firmly or put it off till tomorrow (or never)? How does she react when you discipline the dog? If she comes to its defense when the dog is clearly in the wrong she will do the same with your children undermining your parenting efforts and your authority. If you let the dog out and it runs off and will not come when you call your adolescent children will probably do the same. We could go on and on and on with this however I think you get the point. Think of the dog as a practice child. Raising a puppy requires the same skill set as raising children. It requires equal measures of love, patience and discipline in order for the dog to develop the required behavior to be socialized into the family. If your perspective mate cannot do this with the dog she will not be able to do it with a child either.

Finally remember that children learn primarily by example, you must ask yourself whether your prospective spouse would provide a good example for your children.

Family

It is extremely important to remember that when you get married you are not only marrying your prospective spouse but you're marrying her entire family. This may not be a big issue if you're living thousands of miles away but if you're going to be living near her family they are going to be a big part of your life. If your prospective mate's family is constantly squabbling among themselves you and your wife will be dragged into it sooner or later. The ideal perspective mate will have a happy well-adjusted family that you've spent a lot of time with and that you know well. They should also know you well and approve of you. Parental disapproval of you as a prospective spouse is an ominous sign because it may indicate that your prospective spouse is entering into this relationship is an act of defiance to her parents particularly her father. Anyone who enters into this kind of behavior with their parents will duplicate the behavior with their spouse. Also, a much stronger marriage will result if you actually enjoy the company of her family members. If you dread visiting her parents or spending holidays with her family you can bet you will be miserable in the years to come because she's going to want to do this. You will be expected to participate in the family and if you know in advance this is going to be difficult for you, now is the time to adjust your attitude or invoke the 50 ways.

Just remember blood is thicker than water and any time there's a conflict her family is likely to take her side. Also she will take the side of her family many times rather than that of her spouse. This is why it's important to ascertain before the marriage if there are significant areas of disagreement, which could drive a wedge between you and your spouse in the marriage.

Pets

If you're prospective mate has pets, it's best to understand that you're marrying them to. They will be part of your life and part of your family. If you don't like them or they don't like you there's sure to be trouble. It is important that your perspective mate demonstrate that she understands the difference between people and animals. If not you could just as well find yourself in the doghouse. Unless you want to find yourself treated like a dog, best pick a prospective spouse that understands and respects the difference between her pets and her spouse.

Friends

 Usually after getting married there will be a paradigm shift in the friendships both you and your wife have. You will both be leaving the orbits occupied by your unmarried friends because you will have less and less in common with them. Neither spouse is going to understand if the other spouse continues to socialize with their unmarried friends as if they were still single. Doing this is a recipe for disaster for the marriage and the relationship.

The successful couple will cultivate friendships with other healthy married couples with whom they have more in common. This complicates matters a little bit because there are four personalities involved rather than two. Couple's friends can be an awful lot of fun though and even more satisfying than individual friendships because the couple shares them.

Sexual Attitudes

 Examine carefully the sexual attitudes of your prospective mate. If she has certain practices or inhibitions which are incompatible with your desires this is a set up for conflict later on in the relationship and greatly increases the chances of infidelity on the part of one or both partners. Before getting married is the time for you and your prospective mate to be brutally honest with each other about what excites you sexually and more importantly what does not.

 One needs to be virtually sure that the prospective mate has not pretended to be something she's not in order to take the relationship into the realm of marriage. Literally always once the goal is attained this person will revert to their real attitudes on the subject. This will invariably create a lot of resentment, which may lead to serious problems in the marriage and in the relationship.

Whatever you do, do not expect that long held sexual attitudes, morals or preferred sexual practices will change after the wedding. Remember a leopard does not change its spots. Therefore it's extremely important that every aspect of sexuality be discussed openly and frankly before entering into a marriage. Further you must assure yourself to the extent possible that the information thus obtained is accurate and does not contain misinformation designed to further the relationship by telling you what you want to hear.

Chapter 5

Alternatives to Marriage

"If you are thinking of getting married, just find some snarly bitch that you can't stand and buy her a house instead...you'll be a lot better off in the long run!"

-Anonymous

Are you an Alpha?

Now it's time for you, the reader, to do a little soul-searching. Look at your history with girls. How many partners have you had? If it's a lot, you're probably used to a lot of variety. Are you sure you want to settle down to one woman? Are you **sure** you're able to settle down to one woman?

Usually the first year of marriage is a lot of fun and involves a lot of sex. After a year most couples become somewhat desensitized to the sexual part of the relationship and have to rely on the other aspects of their union to keep them together. If you're a dyed in the wool Alpha, this is probably going to be pretty hard for you. I'm not saying that you can't do it but I am saying that in a weak moment you might succumb to the temptations to be unfaithful.

If you are already looking at other women and fantasizing about them before you're married this will only get worse with time. Telling yourself the truth, if it seems to you that you're likely to be unfaithful to your wife at some point perhaps you should consider taking the Rhett Butler approach admitting to yourself that you're not the marrying kind.

Do the Math

"If it flies, floats or fucks, rent it don't buy it!"
~Anonymous

This could happen to you!

When Tom and Belle's divorce was final and all the financial smoke cleared. Here's how the finances worked out:

One half the community property	*$560,000*
Alimony for 10 years	*$360,000*
Legal expenses	*$315,000*
Jewelry/ Gifts	*$65,000*
Total	*$1,297,000*

During the 10 years they were married, Tom calculated that on room, board, clothing, nails, hair, shelter, *entertainment, medical and dental that he had spent an average of $4,000/ month on Belle. Over 10 years that will amount to $480,000.*

*All total being married to Belle cost Tom **$1,777,000***

*Tom also calculated that during the first eight years of their marriage they had sex on average two times a week. During the last two years of the marriage not at all. That's a total of 832 times during the marriage at an astounding cost of **$2135.81** per time!*

Although Belle was quite attractive and sexy one must admit that that's some ***pretty expensive pussy***. At the trial of Hollywood Madame Heidi Fleiss, Charlie Sheen testified he had paid Fleiss $53,000 for encounters with 27 women for an average price of only $1962.96 per encounter. As you see you can spend the whole night with a call girl or porn star with a centerfold body that's a perfect 10 for less than what Tom paid Belle and she will never bitch at you for forgetting to take out the trash!

What's Love Got to Do With It?

Some of you are probably thinking that the last paragraph was pretty cold and doesn't account for true love. Ask Tom what his true love for Belle cost him. This is probably one of the more important things in this book that the young man must understand. Just because you're in love is no reason to get married. Just think, what if you'd married every girl you had ever been in love with. You'd probably already have 4 to 6 ex-wives by now and your entire paycheck would be taken up just to pay the alimony. One should look at marriage as more of a business proposition than a matter of the heart. I understand that it can be both however you must understand that the business portion of the relationship deserves even more attention than the romantic portion since that part is going to last even past the marriage if it ends in divorce.

One must remember that the earner in the marriage is making a long-term contract to provide for the non-earner even if the marriage is a failure. This obligation goes on long after the marriage has ended.   The non-earner has no obligation whatsoever to the earner. I know it doesn't seem fair but it's the law. This is another good reason to marry someone who makes more than you do. If you do think you found true love just be sure you have read and understood the preceding chapters and followed the advice in the next chapter before you say "I Do."

Living Out of Wedlock

In this day and time, cohabitation has become more or less accepted as a way of life in our society. It is more and more common particularly when one or both of the partners has a high income. One must be sure that it is done in such a way that your spouse does not become eligible to be a common-law wife under the laws of your state.

It is my opinion that at least a year of cohabitation should be undertaken before marriage to be sure that you can live with each other 24/7. In any case: cohabitation should be at least considered as an alternative to marriage particularly if there are misgivings or uncertainties on the part of either partner.

You'll Love the Little Bastards

What about kids? Shouldn't I get married if I want to have kids? Well before you do get married just to have kids be advised that 37% of births in America are to couples that are not married.

If you do decide that you want to have a child out of wedlock be advised that this will irreversibly tie you to the child's mother making you responsible for child support which will amount to anywhere between 14 and 20% of your *gross income*. Then there's always the matter of visitation and if the mother doesn't want to cooperate, or moves away this can mean a lot of legal fees and travel expenses.

So you still want to be married

Well good for you! Read on and decide for yourself if:

(1) You are prepared to settle down and get married.
(2) Your prospective spouse is prepared to settle down and get married.
(3) You've taken the steps necessary to protect yourself from disturbed or predatory females and their divorce lawyers.

Chapter 6

Before the Wedding:

A Checklist

Are you worthy as a couple?

Whatever you may think of the Bible, it is a compendium of time-tested truths of Western Civilization. These truths are not presented literally but rather as an allegory. It is useful at this time to examine what the Bible says God requires of a husband and of a wife. According to the scripture, if the requirements are met God will pour both hearts full of love. The requirements for a husband are much different than those for a wife.

The husband is required to love his wife more than he loves himself and to give his very life if required to protect and defend her. If you don't feel this way about your prospective mate then you're probably not worthy to be her husband an you should consider seriously whether or not you've chosen the right person.

The wife is required to respect and obey her husband. Before going off the deep end over the word "obey" consider this. If the husband has met God's requirement that he love his wife more than himself he would never ask his wife to do something she objected to because his love for her would prevent this. The word respect means to "look again". All this means that the wife is required to respect the sacrifices her husband has made for her and the family and to conduct herself accordingly. If your prospective mate does not respect you, then she is probably not worthy to be your wife.

There's been a lot written about the religious concept of the "Right man-Right woman". Even if you're not the religious type you'll find this concept interesting and the reader is encouraged to investigate it further.

A good place to do this is:

http://www.biblenews1.com/document1.htm - Marriage

This website is a wealth of information about marriage in general and about marriage as it relates to traditional western religion in particular. If you want a marriage that will last, you and your prospective mate should explore the site carefully and evaluate the information as it applies to you. In doing so you may discover something that is invaluable in sustaining a healthy marriage, and that is a spiritual component to the relationship.

An Ounce of Prevention Is Worth a Pound of Cure

"I've had ample contact with lawyers, and I'm convinced that the only fortune they ever leave is their own". ~Wilson Mizner

 The old saying is true, just as your mother told you "**an ounce of prevention is worth a pound of cure**". What follows is your ounce of prevention checklist. Its purpose is to make sure all the conditions are right for you to have a happy marriage and to avoid or at least be prepared for the expensive tragedy of divorce, which is inherently biased against men. The reader is urged to take this exercise seriously. Do it not and you will probably live to regret it.

First Look at Yourself-Got any Red Flags?

 " First to thine own self be true."

 ~ William Shakespeare

 Take a moment and put yourself in your prospective mates shoes. Reread the red flags section and see if you have any of these red flags that would be obvious to her. If there are some things of concern you have to ask yourself "have these potential problems been appropriately addressed?"

If you have a drug or alcohol problem yourself or unresolved mental health issues, prior relationship issues, family issues, or fidelity issues you are unlikely to be able to go forward successfully with your new spouse without solving these first. A good critical look at yourself may reveal that you are not ready for marriage and to press forward knowing this is beyond stupid.

If you have these problems my advice is to find a good therapist and talk it through thoroughly before taking the plunge into marriage. Ignoring this advice will only make the problems you're suffering from worse especially if you're subjected to the financial penalty and stress involved in a divorce.

Maturity

I'm hoping we don't have to consider the question of maturity further but one last warning is in order. In order to be successful in marriage you must be self-actualized, self-sufficient, self-loving, confident, and capable.

You must have considered all the options, and you must have examined the facts carefully while thinking with the big head.

If you have not reached your 30th birthday, *have patience Grasshopper*, it will come. Face not your future until you're ready.

Financial assessment risk-benefit ratio

"Ah, yes, divorce... from the Latin word meaning to rip out a man's genitals through his wallet."

 ~Robin Williams

 You need to put together a little spreadsheet, which includes your income and her income. Then add it altogether and divide by two. If her income is less than yours then subtract her income from this figure and this is about what you'll have to pay in alimony. Oversimplified to be sure but it's a good thumbnail figure to go by. If her income is higher than yours, don't bother. Unless she makes seven figures you'll never get a penny from her. Sorry to be the bearer of bad tidings but as a male you have an inherent disadvantage when it comes to family courts. If the difference figure is small then your risk is small if it's large then your risk is large. In some venues the spouse at fault is destined to be punished even if the difference is small you may find yourself paying more than you expect. The only way to overcome the gender disparity is with a prenuptial agreement. Don't get married without it. More on this later.

Full Disclosure

Before you take a big leap into marriage be sure you have fully disclosed your expectations to your mate.

Let's start with your career. Your new mate should fully understand your goals and the extent to which your attention, your time, your treasure and your energy will be expended towards those goals. You have to be sure that her expectations are reasonable with regard to your aspirations in your career and that she is fully willing to cooperate to achieve the goals you've outlined. Further you need to understand the extent to which she is willing to sacrifice to help you achieve the goals you set for yourself. You also need to make it plain what actions will be required on her part to fulfill your expectations of her performance as your mate. In many cases your mate may be a great asset in the social aspects of your career provided she's willing to cooperate. Just as a cooperative mate can be a great asset an uncooperative one can be a serious liability.

If sacrifices are required, this needs to be abundantly clear prior to marriage. It would be unwise and unfair to enter into a marriage where your mate expects you to work 40 hours a week when in actuality 60 hours a week will be required. These problems are all best dealt with on the front end. It's always best to dial down the expectations to the worst-case scenario. At least if you find yourself in a worst-case scenario you've given full disclosure. If you fare better so much the better because then you have over performed. Performance as promised or over performance is always preferable to underperformance. The take-home message here is to refrain from promising your mate a rose garden that you cannot deliver.

Any foreseeable situation, which you are aware of that may affect your relationship in the future, should be disclosed, fully. No exceptions. The same should hold true for your mate.

Your fiancée

Hopefully you've made an objective assessment of your fiancée paying particular attention to any red flags, which may have been mentioned earlier in this book.

Predatory Females

"Whenever I date a guy, I think, is this the man I want my children to spend their weekends with?"

~Rita Rudner

If your doctor told you that there is a 50% chance that you will need a major operation within the next 2 years, you can bet that you would be sure that your health insurance was in good standing. Well when getting married there is a 50% chance that marriage will end in divorce so don't you think a little insurance is in order here too?

Before you decide to be married be sure the woman you pick is not some sociopath whose plan all along was to take you to the cleaners. Such a woman will have the tools available to her to do just that considering the family law system and divorce industry that presently exists. You must protect yourself on the front end of the process.

 When faced with divorce many women will become vindictive, especially when goaded by their lawyers. Think about this before you say, " I do."

 Becoming pregnant by you is another way for a woman to put you in harness for a quarter of a century. You Alphas think about this before you spread your sperm indiscriminately. It could turn out to be the most expensive piece of ass you ever had.

Some Insurance:

A New Laptop for the One You Love

 If you find yourself this far along in the process still wrestling with worrisome doubts then it's time for you to give your prospective spouse a gift that will keep on giving and at the same time provide valuable insurance should your worst fears come to pass and the whole marriage go to hell in a hand basket.

As I've said before there's nothing more valuable than objective intelligence so it's time to give your spouse a brand-new laptop. This new laptop needs to be fast because it will be running a program in the background. The program I'm speaking of is SpectorPro ($99 from Spectorsoft). With this program installed you can monitor, e-mail, web browsing, instant messaging, chats and a myriad of other important parameters which will give you objective intelligence about online activities should such information be required. Here's the link to the Spector soft website where you can read about the specific capabilities of the program.

http://www.spectorsoft.com/

Whatever you do, tell no one that this program is installed, ever. If it is not needed, leave it un accessed but think of it as insurance in case of infidelity or divorce. Should you become suspicious you can call upon the information as needed. If you find something incriminating, resist the impulse to confront your spouse because in doing so you will cut off a valuable source of information. It may continue to provide you with valuable information even after you are married or during a divorce. It will become obvious to you, as you read on that a tool like this could be invaluable in protecting yourself from predatory females and their attorneys.

Use the information gained to find other ways to discover the truth. For instance, if you discover that she's planning to meet someone at a certain time and place you can arrange to show up there too, as if by accident. Whatever you do try not to compromise the usefulness of this invaluable tool.

Prenuptial Agreement

This could happen to you!

Let's turn back the clock and look at the story of Tom and Belle. At the time of Tom's first divorce he had been working with Belle for almost 2 years. She was married at the time and although their relationship was completely professional by coincidence they found themselves both in the middle of a divorce at the same time. This gave them a lot to talk about and their relationship was born. Having experienced the terrors of divorce Tom was worried that Belle was interested in him mostly for his earning capability. Belle reassured him that she was from a wealthy family and that she was taken care of. After both divorces were final Tom and Belle moved in together. The relationship was sexually charged and Tom could barely wait to get home every evening. After living together for almost a year they began to talk about marriage and children. Remembering his divorce Tom Asked Belle for a prenuptial agreement. She flatly refused. This is when Tom stopped thinking with the bighead. He figured what the hell he loved her and after a year living with her couldn't imagine life without her. More on the divorce later but suffice it to say after Belle and her attorneys were through with Tom, despite the fact that he was still employed as a surgeon, he was living paycheck to paycheck and couldn't even afford needed dental care. This story will be continued in Chapter 9 "Until Divorce Do Us Part ".

This is probably the most important take-home message in the entire book. If your prospective mate/ wife acts like she has something to hide or acts like there's a hidden agenda then there is. Period! And now Tom wishes he'd known about the 50 ways.

Making a prenuptial agreement is quick, easy and you wil learn a lot about your partner in the process. You can hire a lawyer if you wish but this step will definitely complicate the process. The first thing your lawyer will want you to do is hire a second lawyer for her so the two lawyers can play off of each other during the negotiations. Lawyer #1 will put something in which you wil have to pay lawyer #2 to take out.

You and your prospective spouse can do the whole thing on line in less than an hour at:

.http://www.rocketlawyer.com/prenuptial_agreement-form.aspx

You should really do this together so your spouse has some degree of ownership in the resulting document but if worse comes to worse you can do it yourself and have her sign it. Be sure you have a notary and plenty of witnesses to show that she was not forced to sign against her will.

If Ms. Right won't sign a pre-nuptial then it's time to wake-up and smell the coffee, heed the road signs, think with the bighead, see the red flag and invoke the 50 ways!

Grab your hat and run, or if you can't do this and all else fails go back down to the Dew Drop Inn and get another lesson from Bubba. That beating will be nothing compared to the beating you will take when your future ex-wife and her lawyer takes you to the cleaners. Tom learned this lesson the hard way let's hope you don't have to.

Rule #1

No pre-nuptial agreement, no wedding, no exceptions, no excuses, no rationalizations, no quarter asked or given, think with the big head now or suffer the consequences later.

Turn the Page for Rule #2

Refer to Rule #1.

Chapter 7

Living Happily Ever After

Balancing Work and Family

If you have followed the suggestions in the previous chapter you will at least have a wife who has reasonable expectations regarding your work, however this is only half the equation. You need to make a conscious effort not to bring your work home with you if at all possible. In the healthy marriage homecoming of the breadwinner is an important event and a happy family, giggling children and a smiling wife will be your reward. Achieving this requires somewhat of a balancing act where the needs of the family and the needs of the job are reconciled. A cooperative mate makes this a lot easier. One way to ensure your mate's cooperation is through communication.

Debriefing

I recommend a daily ritual, which I like to call "**Debriefing**". This is a period of time chosen by mutual agreement but probably best done immediately upon arriving home. The time required for the debriefing can be anywhere from 10 min. to over an hour. This time needs to be private between husband and wife with no screaming children to interrupt. During this time it is important to discuss the events of the day for each partner, give important notices, sync your schedules and negotiate a division of labor to attend to issues involving everyday life which require periodic action, adjustment or maintenance. It is also important to share both positive and negative events, which affect you personally, as well as the family in general. All this requires a spirit of cooperation between the mates and a great deal frankness and honesty.

You will find your mate to be more cooperative with regard to issues involving your work if she has at least a modicum of understanding concerning what goes on at your job. It will also be very helpful to you to understand what is going on at her job or at home while you're at work.

Finally this is also an important time to strengthen the bond between mates with gestures of reassurance, continuing cooperation and love. This debriefing is really what marriage is all about and it is the foundation upon which a happy life can be built. Both partners must participate, both partners must be frank and honest, both partners must cooperate and both partners must be willing to compromise. This spirit of communication, cooperation, and compromise is the very lifeblood of your marriage. See that you attend to it every single day for the care and feeding of this part of your relationship will likely be the most important determining factor in the outcome of your marriage. Enough said, nothing to think about, *just do it!*

Housewife or Working Mother

"Idle hands are soon turned to the devil's work."
~Anonymous

One of the more important decisions you and your spouse will have to make is whether she will be a housewife or working mother. For financial reasons the latter may be the more practical choice however there are numerous other reasons why making a housewife out of your spouse is a big mistake. It may not be a bad idea for your spouse to be a stay-at-home mom when the child is an infant or for the first two or three years of life. But it is an exceedingly bad idea for her to do this once a child enters preschool or elementary. Often they will spend too much time at the gym, shopping or with their girlfriends and sooner rather than later they will be up to no good. Hanging around with other bored housewives their attention often turns into bitch sessions about how rotten their husbands are. Having no other point of reference soon they begin to believe this even if it's not true.

Further housewives soon become spoiled and too soon forget that everything they have, eat or spend comes from the sweat of their husband's brow. Many will subconsciously feel that their contribution as mother and housewife is inconsequential and may become resentful of their husbands refusing to allow that their husband's hard work entitles them and any special treatment at home. Most husbands who are providing a standard of living, which allows their spouse to be a stay-at-home mom, will be very resentful of being asked to do things at home that the housewife should have done while they were at work. Many housewives will be insistent that after spending the entire day at work the husband is expected do his share of the work that is required in the home. They devalue the work the husband has been doing to support the family. This happens for several reasons, one is, if they acknowledge that the husband spent all day working then they are obliged to provide some quid pro quo when the husband returns home. Another reason is since they are a not contributing to the support of the family financially they subconsciously feel less important; by refusing to recognize the husband's contribution they feel more important by comparison.

Many women once reaching middle age begin to examine the purpose of their life and if it has only been child rearing and homemaking, they often find it lacking.

They will subconsciously blame you for facilitating this by paying all the bills. They may also express resentment towards you for having kept them from "reaching their full potential". Of course this is the equivalent of biting the hand that feeds them but most of them will do this rather than take any responsibility for their lackadaisical approach to life. This is the primary reason why you must not deprive your wife of her self-sufficiency by allowing her to be a stay-at-home mom forever.

So much the better if your wife's earning power is equal to or more than yours, however if she does make more than you, then you will never hear the end of it! Also remember if your spouse is a working mom then you owe it to her to share in the household chores or hire someone else to do them. In a healthy relationship there is a pre-negotiated division of labor, which is agreed to by both parties, and which both parties feel is fair. Without this resentment will raise its ugly head sooner or later and nothing can damage a long-term relationship more.

The Realities of Aging

It is a basic fact of nature that women age more rapidly than men. You see this every day on the street, at Wal-Mart and at the shopping mall. I'm surprised at how many couples that are the same age have such a disparity of appearance. This can cause a giant problem particularly if younger females are attracted to the virility exhibited by a 40 something male. If he's married to a woman the same age her beauty is already waning and she will soon be nearing menopause. The temptation to mate with a younger woman can be overwhelming and the younger women can be quite aggressive when they feel like the object of their desire is married to someone who is over the hill. The only way to combat this is to marry someone younger than you in the first place or resort to plastic surgery.

The Decisions

In every marriage there will be decisions to make which will affect both spouses. If you agree on the decision, then the process is easy. Hopefully you have already negotiated the big foreseeable issues in advance of the wedding. There will eventually be big decisions to be made where the partners can't agree. In this case you will need to negotiate. In this negotiation each spouse must be free to have full expression of their position and their feelings, however the final decision should be made by the spouse that is affected the most, hopefully with consideration of the other spouses feelings and position. For example, if the decision involves your job that affects you the most so the final decision should be yours. On the other hand if the decision involves your wife's family that affects her the most so the final decision should be hers. I understand that both spouses are affected by every decision but usually one spouse will be affected more, whoever is affected more should make the final decision and take the responsibility for it including the responsibility to consider the affect on their spouse.

How to Get the Love You Need

After the book of the same name "**How to get the Love You Need**" by psychologist and author Harville Hendrix. This book should be required reading for all couples contemplating matrimony. In the book Hendrix likens lovers feelings for one another to a bank account. When you do something thoughtful or nice for your partner that's like a deposit. When you do something selfish, inconsiderate, hurtful or rude that's like a withdrawal. If your account becomes overdrawn, you are in trouble.

Reading and understanding this book together will greatly increase your chances of having a happy marriage and a happy life full of love and understanding. Give your spouse a copy of this book and then read and study it together before you wed for a happier healthier marriage.

How to Fight Fair

It goes without saying but in every life some rain must fall. No one should expect to have a relationship devoid of conflict. A relationship is judged not by the presence or absence of conflict but by the way the partners handle the conflict.

As with so many other things pertaining to relationships, timing is everything. Once the respective positions of the partners have been outlined and the parameters of the conflict defined, it is best to take a little time to think about possible solutions. It is ill advised to go forward with discussions, debate or disagreements if one or both of the partners is not intellectually engaged due to their emotional state. Each partner should have the right to call a timeout ranging anywhere from a few minutes to a few hours to ensure that both partners are in control their emotions well enough to have a rational discussion. If one or both partners are in a state of emotional rage then it is unlikely that further discussion will result in anything but a worsening of the conflict. Taking a time out allowing one or both partners to cool off and resuming the discussion at a later time is more conducive to compromise and will likely bring the problem to a better resolution.

This being said it is unwise and hurtful for either partner to storm out. This only widens the gap, which must ultimately be overcome for a harmonious outcome. Both partners should agree before getting married that they will refrain from abandoning each other in times of conflict. It is a childish act to "take your toys and go home" at a time when the partners should be working together to resolve their differences. Storming out when you're angry sends a message that you not do not care about your partner and that you want them out of your life at least temporarily. Staying away overnight is even more ill advised and can cause irreparable damage to the relationship.

Conflicts are resolved by working together as adults to define the issues, work out reasonable compromises and implement agreed-upon solutions. Conflicts are made worse by saying hurtful things, failing to respect your partner, and failing to control your emotions. Abandoning your partner out of anger will always make the problem worse.

Pregnancy Changes

Once pregnant forever fat

It always amazes me how little women are taught about pregnancy. Once pregnant the instinct is to eat everything in the refrigerator, if not everything in the whole house. You know your pregnant spouse is in trouble when she is on a first name basis with the drive-through person at Wendy's. The world is full of beautiful women who got pregnant and for nine months ate everything they could get their hands on gaining a full 60 pounds or more with the pregnancy. After the baby delivered many were surprised to learn that they only lost about 15 of those pounds leaving 45 pounds of ugly fat that in most cases will be there forever.

Just go to Wal-Mart some Friday afternoon and do your own poll. Take account of the women with infants and children under three and you will see at least 60% of them are frankly obese. Now look at their spouses (if they still have one) and you'll see this these men are often thin and attractive. If you didn't know they were married with children you would not expect that this male would have chosen this female for his mate. He didn't, the female that he chose was some 45 pounds thinner when they married.

Nobody told her about the instinct to eat when you're pregnant. This is something you must discuss with your wife before she becomes pregnant and become satisfied that she has a plan to prevent this from happening to her. While she is pregnant you must do everything in your power to prevent her from overeating. This may include getting certain kinds of highly caloric food out of the house. Her instinct is telling her to eat, eat, and eat! And you must tell her that she's had enough, to slow down, to be careful what she eats and keep track of her weight daily. Remember, she shouldn't gain any significant amount of weight for the first trimester. She'll say "I'm eating for two now!" You say "yeah, that's one person and one baby not two people. The baby needs only 300 more calories per day, you have more than that in your hand right now!" During this time you must not tempt her by bringing her favorite foods or playing the pickles and ice cream game. (It's just a rouse to get to the ice cream anyway. The pickles are ok.) She will thank you later if she has half a brain.

Stretch marks

A lot of women have their beauty marred by stretch marks, which were incurred during pregnancy. This is a shame because the problem is mostly preventable. The cause of stretch marks as loss of elasticity of the skin due to dryness, which is made worse in pregnancy. Twice-daily application of <u>Mother's Friend Stretch Mark Cream</u> can prevent this ugly side effect of pregnancy. Be sure your spouse has plenty of mothers friend available to her at all times particularly after the first trimester of pregnancy. She will thank you later.

Breasts

Breasts can easily become another casualty of pregnancy because they are also subject to stretch marks. If the baby is breast-feeding this can become even more of a problem particularly if breast-feeding is done for extended periods of time. To me there's nothing more unsavory than to see a toddler who should be on solid food demanding to be breast-fed. If your spouse is going to breast-feed it probably shouldn't be continued beyond six months. Usually mothers that want to breast-feed for longer than this are more concerned about their own feelings about this than they are their children's best interest. In my opinion infants should start weaning when they begin teething or about 4 months.

Once breast-feeding is over the breast tissue can collapse causing breasts that were previously voluptuous to become pendulous. This is called empty sac syndrome and can be easily remedied by breast augmentation. If you're going to go the breast augmentation route be sure childbearing is finished before you do this.

Roadmap to pregnancy

The first trimester pregnancy begins about two weeks before the first missed menstrual period, which should be roughly the time of conception. Usually this is a time of great joy for the couple especially if the event has been planned. During the first trimester of pregnancy your spouse will experience morning sickness to a greater or lesser degree. This can be a very trying time for some women and is very important for you to be understanding and tolerant as a husband.

Second trimester begins about 13 weeks and will usually be accompanied by a decrease in the more unpleasant symptoms experienced during the first trimester. Most couples will experience an increase in libido during this time, which can be very satisfying for both partners. Also during the second trimester the woman will experience an increase in appetite and an instinct to increase her caloric intake. As described before most women will have a tendency to go overboard with this and must be reminded that the baby only needs an additional 300 cal per day.

In the third trimester the growth of the fetus accelerates and most Women will experience some mood swings and some emotional instability. The diligent husband will take this into consideration and show his wife his devotion by being as caring and understanding as possible during this time. Just prior to delivery many women will show a sudden burst of energy, deciding to clean out the garage or undertake some other large project, which in her condition may be ill advised. If you see this in your spouse late in the third trimester discourage her from undertaking this task and remember it probably means the delivery is imminent.

Changes with the Little Bundle of Joy

One of the biggest changes, which will come about after the baby is delivered, is a refocusing of energies and attentions on the newest member of the family. Where before you only had each other to take care of now there's a helpless third person whose needs must be met. Some spouses can become overwhelmed with all this new responsibility. As the husband you must be prepared to provide her with everything she needs to take care of the baby. This may include help from a housekeeper or nanny until she can get back on her feet.

Also during this time one must be very careful to look for the signs of postpartum depression, which can be very severe and even result in suicide if unrecognized. If your spouse is not eating, not sleeping, sleeping too much, disinterested, or downright blue you should consult your doctor immediately. Postpartum depression is caused from the rapid reduction in hormone levels and has little if anything to do with your spouse's pre morbid psychiatric condition. You may be the only one present who is capable of recognizing this condition. It is imperative that it be treated promptly.

Care and Feeding of a Relationship with Children

Once your relationship settles into a routine, which involves childcare and refocuses the attention of both spouses on the needs of the children it becomes of paramount importance to see that the couple has at least some time to keep the romantic part of their relationship alive. One good thing to do is to be sure that both spouses have something to look forward to such as a date night at least every two weeks, which does not include the children. If your spouse is unwilling or unable to engage alternate childcare during these times, take the bull by the horns and do it yourself. If you have a romantic relationship you must use it or lose it.

Also at least a couple of times a year you and your spouse should engage in a romantic weekend away again without the children.

This could happen to you!

When Bill and Edna's first child was 14 months old they had a chance to go to Orlando for a meeting Bill needed to attend. Bill wanted Edna to a company him since he would have plenty of time between meetings to explore the attractions. Although Edna's mother was perfectly willing to care for the child Edna insisted on bringing the child along.

The flight was uncomfortable for the baby because he was unable to equalize the pressure in his ears. On the second day of the trip Bill and Edna packed the baby in a backpack on Bills back and headed out for the Magic Kingdom. One older gentleman commented to them rather boldly that they should have left that baby at home. Despite the extra trouble having the baby along entailed they still had an enjoyable day at the park.

Later that night the baby came down with a fever, which proved to be rather hard to control. Both Bill and Edna were terrified when the baby suffered a febrile seizure in the hotel room. They rushed the baby to the hospital where they spent most of the night waiting for the child who eventually left the emergency room under his own power at about four o'clock in the morning.

Bill and Edna spent an agonizing 12 hours in airports and flying back home. Once home they took the baby to his own pediatrician who diagnosed an inner ear infection probably due to the airline flight. As it turned out the nosy old man at Disneyland was absolutely right. The baby didn't remember much about the trip to Disneyland but he remembered every detail about the emergency room.

The story points out in some detail the unintended consequences that can come about when one exercises poor judgment based upon their emotions. Bill and Edna should have gone to Disneyland by themselves and waited until the child was old enough to enjoy it to take him there.

The Marital Bed

Do not under any circumstances permit your children to sleep in the marital bed. You will end up not getting a good nights sleep and further it will be a struggle to get them back into their own bed when it becomes necessary. The child sleeping in the marital bed greatly interferes with any intimacy that might occur otherwise. Your spouse may want to do this out of convenience so that she does not have to get up during the night. However the child will become accustomed to sleeping with other people and there will be a fit when you try to put them in his or her own bed. The struggle can go on for years and it is best not to get it started in the first place. Put your foot down from the beginning and insist that the child sleep in his own bed even as an infant. If a child needs to be close to the parents because of illness or for other reasons simply bring the crib into your bedroom not the baby into your bed.

Living Happily Ever After

One of the problems with living happily ever after is to devise a way to keep from falling into a routine and becoming bored. This is especially true when you have children. It is your job as head of the household to see the appropriate activities are planned so that all members of the household have something to look forward to, to prevent boredom.

All members of the household do not have to participate in every activity and particular attention has to be given to the relationship between spouses so that It remains exciting and engaging. Hopefully by the time your relationship gets to this point you're not only lovers but also best friends. Add a satisfying sexual relationship and a healthy respect for your spouse to this and you have all the makings of living happily ever after.

Another thing that you can do while living happily ever after is to make sure the to celebrate all the holidays making sure that you make every effort to make them festive. This will not only build memories between you and your family but also between you and your mate making the family unit stronger and more resilient to the stresses and strains of everyday life. Each upcoming holiday will give the family something to look forward to especially if they know that you're committed to making the experience a memorable one.

Above all this means spending quality time with your mate and making an effort to keep the romance in the relationship alive.

Chapter 8

When There's Trouble in Paradise

Infidelity

After reading the chapter on the biology of love and mating the astute reader would conclude that humans are not hardwired particularly well for monogamy.   In fact in the real world most relationships could best be described as linear polygamy. This is certainly borne out by the statistics.   One or both spouses admit to infidelity in 41% of marriages. 57% of males and 54% of females admit to having been unfaithful to their mates at some time in life. 74% of males and 68% of females say that they would have an extramarital affair if they knew they would never get caught.

The average duration of an extramarital affair is two years. There are several peak times in a marriage when the likelihood of infidelity is increased. After the first year of marriage is one of those times. This is the time when one or both partners have become somewhat desensitized to the sexual and emotional high that they experienced during the first year of their marriage. Review the section in chapter 2 on the chemistry of love to better understand this phenomenon. Usually affairs occurring after the first year of marriage are not serious but rather just a sexual fling to reassure the person that they're still attractive to the opposite sex. However as I've said before in this book " Once an adulteress always an adulteress." Adultery is always a serious matter.

The second time in a marriage where the risk of infidelity increases is after the first child is born. A child always brings with it new responsibilities and causes the marriage to focus on the third person rather than on each other. Like in the first year of marriage, infidelity of the wife after the first child is born often relates to her need to be seen as sexy and attractive after having had a child. She may not be getting this from her husband because of the physical changes pregnancy has brought about in her.

The most dangerous time of all is the time of the seven-year itch. By this time most couples have bought a home, had one or more children and have pretty much settled into the routine of every day life having achieved the American dream. Unless precautions are taken, one or both partners may become unhappy or bored. Many couples will buy something like a new house or new car or even decide to have another baby to create some excitement. This is a time when both partners should realize that marriage is hard work and that if you don't continue to work hard at it, all may be lost.

As in the story of Frank and Belle, the midlife crisis can also be a very dangerous time. By this time the children are much more self-sufficient and particularly women who've been primarily homemakers begin to question the purpose of their life. As in the case of Belle they might start exercising, by some sexy new clothes, and start spending more time with their divorced girlfriends. The main problem here is that they feel they're losing their edge and because of the aging are now less attractive. An affair is a good way to get an artificial infusion of self-esteem.

This Could Happen to You!

Bill and Edna have been married for seven years. They have a three-year-old son and Bill has an excellent job earning well into the six-figure range. It's Thanksgiving Day and the extended family is getting together at Bill and Edna's for a traditional dinner. Bill is confused because he cannot figure out why Edna is acting the way she is. Their usually warm relationship has suddenly turned cold and uncaring. To Bill this seemed to have happened overnight. Bill approached Edna and asked her if she loved him. Edna replied "not very much." Bill was shocked he'd never seen Edna act like this as long as they had been married. Throughout the day everything seemed relatively normal except for the fact that Edna was giving him the cold shoulder. Bill tried several times to talk about this but she brushed him off every time. Later that evening after Edna went to bed Bill stayed up trying to think what he might've done that made Edna treat him in this way. He could think of nothing that might explain Edna's strange behavior. Finally in desperation he decided to make a hard target search of Edna's car while she was sleeping. He looked at every receipt every piece of paper in the car. Edna wasn't very good at keeping the car clean so there was plenty to look at. Then something Bill found gave him the shock of his life. Hidden between the seats of the car was a folded piece of paper that contained a poem. It was addressed to Edna comparing her to a little bird caught in a cage (an obvious reference to her marriage to Bill). The poem was quite good and quite romantic. It was obvious to Bill that Edna was having an affair. This was the last thing that Bill might have expected. Bill took the poem and copied it replacing the original where he had found it.

The next day Bill called his attorney and was shocked to hear the realities of divorce in his state. Bill decided to collect more evidence so he put a recorder on the phone. He was shocked to hear that Edna and one of her old boyfriends were planning how they were going to divide up everything Bill had worked for the last 10 years. Bill was furious. At least he had them dead to rights.

Not surprisingly, Edna's old boyfriend was still married as well. Bill confronted Edna with the facts and was surprised to learn that Edna wanted to divorce and marry her old boyfriend.

Not wanting a messy divorce, Bill resigned himself to let Edna go quickly in return for favorable property settlement. To their credit they did it with one lawyer and signed the papers at the dining room table. The whole process took less than three months.

Before the ink on the divorce was dry, Edna's old boyfriend hit the road leaving her high and dry. Edna tried everything she could think of to get back with Bill. But Bill wisely refused to re conciliate. We will come back to Bill and Edna's story later.

A lawyer is never entirely comfortable with a friendly divorce, anymore than a good mortician wants to finish his job and then have the patient sit up on the table.
~Jean Kerr

Trust is a lot like Humpty Dumpty, after a fall, all the kings' horses and all the kings' men can't put it back together again. And Edna learned the hard way that you only get one chance at trust, violate it even once and it's lost forever. As well it should be: fool me once shame on you, fool me twice shame on me. Less than 30% of marriages with any history of infidelity will survive.

The time to find out about an affair is not when you stumble on it by accident. One should always be very observant of their spouse particularly if she seems to be depressed or bored. If the relationship is at one of the critical times described above one must be even more vigilant, particularly around time of the ovulation (14 days following the start of menstruation).

Some of the signs that your spouse may be having an affair are:

1) A sudden improvement in mood or outlook on life.
2) Constantly late.
3) More possessive toward her cell phone, wallet, laptop or briefcase.
4) Starts talking about getting together with old friends she hasn't seen in years.
5) New clothes or outfits.
6) Renewed interest in appearance.
7) Keeps an overnight bag or gym bag in her car or office.
8) Works late or on holidays or weekends.
9) Takes new interest in your schedule.
10) Encourages you to visit family or friends alone.
11) Keeps her car free of things belonging to you or the kids.
12) Starts attending extended seminars or conventions particularly out of town.
13) Remembering things she forgot to do at the office at odd hours.

14) Forgets to wear wedding ring.
15) Odd or late night phone calls.
16) Takes up new hobbies or friends that take her out of the house in the evenings or on weekends.
17) Insists on answering the phone.
18) Calling you by the wrong name in sleep.
19) Smell of different soap on returning home.
20) Uses a prepaid calling card or cell phone.
21) Starts exercising or losing weight.
22) Change in her music interests.
23) Accuses you of getting into her things.
24) An increase in the use of ATM.
25) Invents excuses to get out of the house.
26) Carries toothpaste, toothbrush or mouthwash.
27) Becomes friends with people who are going through divorce.
28) Loses interest in sex.
29) Becomes hypersexual.
30) Taking phone calls out of your hearing distance.
31) Accuses you of having an affair.

There are of course many others, but your best weapon is your gut. Your gut instinct will give you the best information on the status of your relationship and will give the best clues to the presence of an extramarital affair. These things are, of course, all subjective and therefore of little use when you need concrete information.

"All's fair in love and war," ~ *Francis Edward Smedley*

And you would be well advised to remember that this is both, particularly if your marriage ends in divorce.

If you feel like your spouse is having an affair then you owe it to yourself and to her to discover the facts. There are many ways to do this some of which may seem a little unsavory. The importance of objective intelligence outweighs any rights to privacy your spouse may have when it comes to an extramarital affair. Without any evidence, as the male, you will be at a terrible disadvantage in a divorce.

When investigating, start with the easy things first. Take a good long look at the cell phone bill. Remember as with the story of Frank and Belle that there may be good reasons for multiple calls to coworkers and others. When investigating these matters you must always be sure to give your spouse the benefit of the doubt and not to jump to conclusions.

Bank Account

Take a line item look at the bank account for transactions that may raise a red flag. If you don't do this already you should probably start even if you don't suspect your spouse of infidelity. Many wives that are planning a divorce will go to great lengths to collect money a little bit at a time. One way they can do this without getting caught is to buy something with a debit card or check and then promptly return it receiving a refund in cash. Numerous ATM withdrawals also indicate the she doesn't want a record of what she is doing with that money.

Physical Evidence

Most people who are having an affair subconsciously want to be caught and will leave plenty of physical evidence everywhere. Do not forget to look for physical evidence in her car, her purse and among her personal effects.

You will be totally shocked what you will learn about your spouse's life by simply going through the trash one piece at a time. It only stands to reason that things she might not what you to see will end up in the trash. It's a disgusting job but somebody has to do it especially if that somebody wants to find out what his spouse is up to.

Electronic Surveillance

E-mail, twitter, Face book and other electronic media outlets may also be hints to what's going on.

If you have given your wife a laptop with appropriate software installed as suggested earlier in this book, that investment will pay off now and this process will be a lot easier.

Monitoring your wife's telephone conversations may be quite time-consuming and sometimes downright boring but as in the case of Bill and Edna it can provide vital information that can change your approach to your marriage. Monitoring is easy on the home phone but also possible on cell phones.

Testing your wife's fidelity

One way of testing your wife's fidelity is to find out what she's up to when you're at work or otherwise occupied. There are a number of technological devices, which will help you with this quest. There are number of GPS devices which operate over the Internet through a cell phone connection which can be placed in or on her car. Her activities and whereabouts throughout the day can be easily traced on the web. If she has a smart phone some of the phones can be equipped with an application which will make her whereabouts available on the web as well. The phone is probably a better option since she may not be using her own car for her philandering.

Here are just a few links to some websites that provide software that will allow you to monitor a smart phone for calls, text, email, just about anything and it's perfectly legal. Also you will be able to find the latest hardware for GPS Tracking and other surveillance tasks.

http://www.CellSpyNow.com

http://www.E-Stealth.com

There are number of companies on the Internet that provide semen detection kits. Samples can be collected from your wife's soiled clothing for testing for the presence of semen. You can identify the parts of the clothing to be tested by examining them under ultra violet light. Any biological material left on the clothing will fluoresce and can easily be identified.

If you find you're having difficulty getting access to your wife's soiled clothing because she washes them before they can be examined this is a good sign that you may find something on them. A good way to gain access to the soiled clothing before it is washed is to turn off the water supply to the washing machine. When she puts her clothing in and tries to start the cycle the machine will give her an error message that she will have no earthly idea what to do about. She will then call you at which time you will pull the machine out and pretend to work on it until she loses interest. At which time you will have access to the clothing you need. If your wife is the technical type you may want to be sure that the manual for the machine is not readily available.

Samples collected can also be tested for DNA so that the supplier of the semen can be positively identified.

Here's another helpful link for the home detection of cheating spouses:

http://www.brickhousesecurity.com/catch-a-cheater.html

As a last resort there is the expensive option of hiring a private investigator. If you think your relationship may end up in a divorce I highly recommend that you bite the bullet and hire the investigator and find out what's going on in advance of starting the process.

Chapter 9

Till Divorce do Us Part

"A divorce is like an amputation: you survive it, but there's less of you. "   *~Margaret Atwood*

The Divorce Industry

"What a holler would ensue if people had to pay the minister as much to marry them as they have to pay a lawyer to get them a divorce." *~Claire Trevor*

There were 1,530,000 divorces in the year 2009. The average combined cost of a divorce for both parties (which the husband usually has to pay) is $30,000. This makes the divorce industry in the United States worth about $45.9 billion annually, the lion's share of this paid to lawyers. On average a divorce costs about one third of the couple's net worth. Since the lawyers have access to all your financial information they know just how much to charge.

Government figures show annual child support payments received by women amount to over $3 Billion dollars. Economist Robert Willis calculated that only one-fifth to one-third of child support payments are used by or for the children; the rest is profit for the custodial parent.

80% of all divorces are unilateral, meaning that only one party wants a divorce while the other wants to stay married. When children are involved the woman more commonly files the complaint.

A father who's done nothing wrong can be forced into a divorce court and deprived of his children, his income, his savings, his home and even his freedom.

Lawyers

"Of course I've got lawyers. They are just like nuclear weapons, I've got em 'cause everyone else has. But as soon as you use them they screw everything up."
~Danny DeVito

The big problem with picking lawyers is that you don't find out whether you've got a good one or not until it's too late.

This could happen to you!

During Tom and Belle's divorce the issue of the valuation of the house came up in court. The judge was looking at the appraisal Tom had submitted which was current. Bell's lawyer argued that a less current appraisal, 8 months old, which valued the house $100,000 more than the current appraisal be used. While this was happening Tom's lawyer was sitting at his desk reading a magazine. Tom felt that at $200 an hour his lawyer should been paying more attention. The judge actually said on the record "I'm no good at math." Tom was aghast but having already been told to keep quiet he said nothing. As it turned out the judge was absolutely right, he was no good at math. When the house finally sold the sales price was $130,000 less than the judge had valued the house. This meant that Tom had to pay Belle $65,000 that she wasn't really entitled to had the assets been valued fairly. By overvaluing the house the judge had given Belle the entire equity, leaving Tom with nothing.

Tom's lawyer advised that the decision be appealed. While the appeal is pending Tom's lawyer told him that the judge had said to him "I learned something from you on this case, I got myself emotionally involved, from now on if the parties can't agree on the value of the home I'll order it sold." Tom was outraged to hear the judge had let his emotions interfere with the decision at hand and further outraged that the judges education cost him $65,000 but Tom's lawyer told him not to worry, the judge will be overturned on appeal just fork over another

$3500 to me and I'll get that appeal on the way.

When the appeal came in Tom was shocked to learn that the judge's decision had been upheld. When Tom asked his lawyer how this could happen the lawyer replied, "Most of the appellate judges don't really like doctors."

When the house finally sold, Tom was almost $40,000 short of the $65,000 that he still owed Belle. By the time this fiasco is over the toll it was taking on Tom caused him to lose his job. Tom's contract called for a separation payment, which Belle's lawyer promptly garnished. Tom found himself without a job and only what was left in his retirement account to live on. Tom was furious with his attorney and couldn't see how any of this could have turned out worse. When Tom's attorney found out he'd been laid off, he promptly resigned leaving Tom without representation.

Tom considered making an ethics complaint but dropped the idea when he discovered that Belle's lawyer was the chairman of the ethics committee.

 Like so many other things having to do with lawyers the game is pretty much rigged to their advantage. Similar scenarios play out every single day across the nation. If you're depending on getting fair treatment from the legal system in a divorce you're a fool.

A fool and his money will soon be parted.
~Anonymous

Lawyer joke:

An Islamic terrorist managed to gain access to the courthouse and took all the lawyers and judges hostage. His demands were as follows: "Until Khalid Sheikh Mohammed is released, I will free one hostage every hour. ALA Akbar!"

Hell Hath No Fury Like a Woman Scorned

"There are four stages in a marriage. First there's the affair, then the marriage, then children and finally the fourth stage, without which you cannot truly know a woman, the divorce." ~Norman Mailer

Since the divorce is an adversarial process it is to the lawyers best advantage if the couple is fighting. And you can be sure that most successful divorce attorneys are experts at manipulating their clients fear, jealousy, arrogance, lust, insecurity and anger. As these emotions are stirred they begin to control the clients thinking and the couple often becomes deadlocked in a battle to destroy each other emotionally, professionally, and economically. Once the conflict gets to this level both attorneys smile because they know they'll be busy for the duration maximizing the billing potential of the case. This will cost you between $200-400 and hour and double that when the attorneys are talking to each other. Should the assets of the couple become exhausted the lawyers will quickly lose interest in this strategy.

Like Beelzebub, any successful divorce attorney will be particularly adroit at arousing the emotion of jealousy. It doesn't matter whether there's another woman or not, a good attorney will convince your soon to be ex-wife that surely there is another woman he just can't prove it. In Tom and Belles divorce, Bell spent thousands and thousands of dollars having Tom followed everywhere by private detectives. This of course was at the advice of her attorney. Since Tom wasn't having an affair it profited Belle nothing, it cost her nothing either since Tom ended up paying all the bills.

 Another thing lawyers love to convince their clients of is that their spouses are somehow hiding money. This makes the client less willing to negotiate a settlement and drive the matter further into litigation. This is just another way of churning the account to maximize legal fees.

If you are in a continuous divorce, another onslaught you can expect to suffer is assignation of your character. You can bet you will be portrayed as a lying, child molesting, alcoholic, drug addicted, cross-dressing, homosexual, Nazi war criminal that cheats on his wife and his taxes and steals from the poor box at the church. It really doesn't matter if this is true or not, they won't need a shred of evidence to get it in the record. The accusation alone will do the damage they intend.

Lawyer joke:

Two lawyers are driving down the road at high speed and they pass beautiful young women walking along the road completely naked.

Lawyer number one slams on the brakes and says, "Did you see that? Let's go back and screw her!"

Lawyer number two said, " Out of what?"

Donkey Pong for Attorneys

"A countryman between two lawyers is like a fish between two cats."
~ Benjamin Franklin

The thing divorce lawyers love to do is a variation of the game of ping-pong (albeit with highly modified rules) which I call donkey-pong. Imagine a game of ping-pong in which the two players each have a manager. One point is awarded to each player that strikes the ball (one point is equal to .25 billable hours). If one player misses the ball, no matter, he will pick up another point when he serves it back to the other player. The game goes on until both players are exhausted. The game ends only if the one of the managers gives up or the money runs out.

When this happens the players high-five and exclaim "WE WON!" and this is where the donkey comes in, that being you the breadwinner of the family. At the end of the game the donkey pays each player his fee for .25 billable hours (the minimum charge for any contact) times the number points each player has accumulated. The longer the game lasts the more points each player will accumulate and the more money they will collect at the end. The more emotional and angry the managers become, the longer the game will go on and the more the donkey that's carrying the whole road show on his back will have to pay.

Lawyer joke:

There once was a lawyer who was run over by a garbage truck. He died and went to heaven. When he got there God himself was standing at the pearly gates. God said to him " To tell the truth, I usually don't meet new arrivals at the gate." The lawyer said, "Why did you make an exception this time?" God replied, "I just wanted to see for myself what a man who lived 214 years looked like." The lawyer looked puzzled and said "I'm just 39." "Oh", God said, " My mistake, I was going on your billable hours."

Child Custody

"Children must be considered in a divorce; considered valuable pawns in the nasty legal and financial contest that is about to ensue." ~P. J. O'Rourke

This Could Happen to You!

After Bill and Edna's reasonably civilized divorce, Bill started new relationship fairly quickly with Marie. After Edna's lover hit the road she quickly decided that she needed to be back with Bill. Bill of course would have none of it not only did he not trust Edna but he was quite happy with this new relationship with Marie. Eventually Marie and Bill moved in together which drove Edna wild with jealousy. And to get back at Bill, Edna began interfering with Bill's visitation of their son Cameron. Bill would come to pick Cameron up at the appointed time to find no one home. The visitation schedule had been set out clearly in the divorce papers however Edna refused to follow it. She also been began criticizing Bill and Marie to Cameron.

When Marie and Bill decided to get married, matters became much worse. When Marie became pregnant the whole big mess went to hell in a hand-basket. Edna was totally uncooperative with anything Bill wanted to do involving Cameron.
She made all manner of accusations as to what happened when Cameron did come to visit. She accused Cameron of loving Marie more than he loved her. Edna

hired a lawyer and filed an action to increase the agreed-upon child support by almost 100%. For Bill this was the last straw. He answered by filing a petition to gain custody. Cameron, who was now nine, seemed to have a lot of problems which included problems in school, obesity, behavior problems and other concerns too numerous to mention here. The action dragged out almost 3 years and the attorney's fees just on Bill's side exceeded $30,000. Bill felt that this action was necessary to save the child from Edna's wrath. Because of some of the bizarre things Edna had done, the judge ordered a psychiatric evaluation of the entire family. The psychiatrist felt that Edna was a borderline personality disorder and recommended that custody be switched from her to Bill.

Having no other option Edna agreed for Bill to become the custodial parent with the concession that she would be spared having to pay child support and have a generous visitation schedule.

At age 12 Cameron moved in with his father, Marie and his now two-year-old half-brother. Times were rough in the beginning because Cameron had no idea how to behave in a household where there were some rules in place. For instance Bill insisted that Cameron do his homework, which was somewhat of a new concept for him. Cameron was uncomfortable with the idea that he should take some responsibility for his life and for his education much preferring the more liberal atmosphere at his mom's. Edna continued to manipulate Cameron and tried to convince him that he would be better off with her.

Believe it or not this story becomes even more incredible in the pages ahead.

All Rise, And Then Bend Over.

"Absolute power corrupts absolutely" ~ Lord Acton

Judges

Probably the most powerful position in the judiciary is the position of Chancellor. This is the judge who will likely preside over any divorce case. They have the power to separate you from your children, take away your property, and confiscate your income. They can also incarcerate and hold you without a trial even when you haven't done anything wrong. Unfortunately Lord Acton was right because chancellors are often narcissistic, self-aggrandizing, self-important, and downright rude.

"Judges are the weakest link in our system of justice, and they are also the most protected."
~Alan Dershowitz

A judge in this kind of position is rarely required to answer to anyone. If he makes an unfair ruling you can bet it will cost you tens of thousands of dollars to appeal it. Even then it is unlikely that the ruling will be reversed and even if it is, nothing of any consequence will happen to the judge who issued it. And you will still be out the cost of the appeal.

"Unfortunately, what many people forget is that judges are just lawyers in robes. "
~Tammy Bruce

A lot of the positions judges take and the rulings they make are designed to uphold the status quo in the divorce industry. In most cases their first concern will be that the lawyers are all paid, well paid.

"It is unfair to believe everything we hear about lawyers, some of it might not be true."
~Gerald F. Lieberman

Not all judges are corrupt just like not all lawyers are unethical. But if they are corrupt, unethical, incompetent or biased then any concept of justice goes out the window. The worst part of the whole thing is that if you find yourself under the thumb of a corrupt, unethical, incompetent or biased judge there's pretty much nothing you can do about it. You can of course file a motion to have the judge recuse himself but the judge in question is the one who's going to decide. Any lawyer will tell you that it practically takes an act of Congress to get a particular judge off a particular case.

Lawyer joke:

The Pope and his lawyer were crossing the street at the Vatican and were run over by the Pope Mobile. Upon arriving in heaven they were greeted by St. Peter who welcomed them and asked them to accompany him so he could show them where they would be spending eternity. The three walked down a long beautiful road and came to a small cottage nestled into the landscape. St. Peter said "Here your Holiness, this is where you will be spending eternity." The Pope said, "It's lovely I'm sure I'll be very happy there thank you very much." Then St. Peter turned to the lawyer and said "If you'll come with me I'll show you where you will be spending eternity." They continued down the lovely road and rising in the distance was a beautiful castle, sparkling crystal spires rising to the clouds. At least 100 angels were assembled on the front steps singing an angelic chorus of welcome. The lawyer was stunned. Every where servants were stirring about making last-minute preparations for the arrival of the castle's new Lord and Master. The lawyer said "Oh St. Peter I don't deserve this. Just let me live in the little cottage down the road and let his Holiness live here." "Oh no," said St. Peter " Here in Heaven Popes are dime a dozen, but *lawyers on the other hand......*"

This Could Happen to You!

 Let go back to the story of Edna and Bill. After Bill got custody of Cameron he began doing better in school and after a period of time things begin to straighten out for him. After about a year living with Bill and Marie Cameron seemed to be getting his life together. For the first time his homework is getting done and he was responsible for some chores around the house. Just as things were going well however Bill's life circumstances changed. It became necessary for Bill to change jobs and move to another state. Bills lawyer told him this would be no problem that all he had to do was give Edna two weeks notice. Bill did as the lawyer instructed, but on the day the moving van arrived Bill got word that Edna had called an emergency hearing and got custody switched back to her. Bill and Marie were committed to the new job and were forced to head off without Cameron.

 Bill was furious with his lawyer and fired him on the spot. Once Bill and Marie were settled they researched the subject carefully and hired another Lawyer who was a child custody expert. With the new lawyer on the job it wasn't long before Bill and Edna were able to bring Cameron to their new home for a visit. While there Cameron admitted that he had not wanted to move and bragged that he and Edna had talked to one of their neighbors who was also a Chancellor in the same county.

After spending $30,000 to gain custody of Cameron now he was facing the prospect again due to illegal and unethical ex parte communications between one of Edna's neighbors and the judge in their case. The new lawyer turned out to be one in a million and went to the Chancellor who had intervened and ask him to his face if he had done this. Not knowing what evidence the lawyer had, he admitted to communicating with the judge assigned to Bill's case on the matter. The lawyer's next stop was a visit to the judge himself. He told the judge that he knew there'd been ex parte communication and asked the judge to step aside, which by some miracle he did. So far Bill and Marie had spent another $10,000 just to get rid of the unethical judge.

It took two years and another $20,000 to regain custody of Cameron. By the time this case wound its way through the courts Cameron was already almost 15 and angry. Bill and Marie did the best they could with Cameron but they soon found out that an angry 15-year-old could affect their marriage as well.

Just before Cameron turned 17 Bill took the whole family on vacation and on return found Sheriff's deputies at their home with one of Cameron's friends under arrest in the back seat. The home and been burglarized and approximately $20,000 worth of electronics, computers, guns, and jewelry had been taken. The Sheriff's *investigation revealed that there were four adults and three juveniles involved. Two days later the deputy returned and to Bill and Marie's horror, arrested Cameron as an accomplice in the burglary. They had plenty of notes and plenty proof that Cameron had helped plan the burglary. Since he was not yet 17 he was charged as a juvenile. Marie never trusted Cameron again, neither did Bill for that matter. It seemed to them that Edna had raised a sociopath, despite Bill's best efforts.*

After spending almost $60,000 to gain custody of Cameron, the $5000 Bill had to pay to the lawyer to defend Cameron added insult to injury. The day Cameron turned 18 he walked out of Bill and Marie's life never to be seen again. Years later Edna called Bill, Cameron was in trouble again and this time was going to jail. She admitted that what she'd done with Cameron was wrong and that her hatred for Bill had destroyed their child.

"Justice delayed is justice denied" ~ William Gladstone

It is notable that Bill was able to find an able and ethical lawyer. It took a tremendous amount of courage for this lawyer to face not one but two judges with allegations of ethical violations. Rest assured you would be lucky to find a lawyer like that but don't hold your breath.

This story also demonstrates that the battle often goes on for years after the divorce. Most fathers do not find as much justice as Bill did, and even then the delay in implementation of the solution caused a dreadful outcome for everyone involved. In the absence of some grievous flaw in the mother, the chances of gaining custody of your children are slim to none. This fact puts the state in your place as father to your children and judges in family court often attempt to micromanage family affairs replacing the values of the parents with their own.

The Human Cost of Divorce

It should be obvious to the astute reader that the process of divorce is both brutal and expensive. In most states the battle will take place over a period of 1-2 years during which time both parties will experience suffering on a monumental scale. During this time lives are put on hold, fortunes decimated, careers ruined, families torn apart, and dreams shattered. Even after the process is over the hatred and resentment generated will continue to affect the lives of the principals far into the future. If you add child custody issues to the process it can last decades depending on the age of the children involved.

Unfortunately the process is particularly unforgiving of any incapacity or neglect and virtually devoid of any compassion for human suffering. The divorce industry is primarily responsible for this travesty and as of this writing the only way to avoid its ravages is to avoid divorce in the first place. The author hopes that the reader has found this book useful in achieving that end.

Chapter 10

Epilogue

Many readers may find themselves in a dilemma at this point. Having read and understood the red flags they now realize that not one of the prospective mates they have been exposed to can make the grade. Or they realize that they themselves are poorly prepared to embark on the journey of marriage. Now what? If you find yourself is this situation, don't give up. Hopefully by now the reader understands the draconian monstrosity that is divorce and further understands that it is to be avoided at all costs. Re-read the section on Alternatives to Marriage and satisfy yourself with that unless and until you find someone worthy and/or get yourself together. Do not under any circumstances take the John Paul Jones approach of "Damn the torpedoes, full speed ahead!" This would be the same as reading all the signs, throwing rocks at them and then going the wrong way. This is just what the divorce lawyers are hoping and praying that you will do. Be strong, be true to yourself and don't fall into this trap.

 It is hoped that the preceding pages have shown that men in general are at a terrible disadvantage in a divorce. It should be clear that neither the court nor the constitution will afford you equal protection under the law. The only hope is for you to protect yourself by choosing your mate wisely, vetting her carefully, obtaining a pre nuptial agreement, taking all reasonable precautions and then taking whatever steps are necessary to keep the marriage healthy and happy. If a divorce then becomes inevitable, have the courage to take those steps required to protect your rights, your treasure, your heart and your children.

For more information or to correspond with the author please visit the website:

http://www.lovemarriagedivorce4men.com

ABOUT THE AUTHOR

The author is a physician and surgeon who has practiced medicine for over 30 years. During this time he devoted considerable time and energy to the compassionate care of his patients. It is equally important to note that he devoted just as much care and energy to his efforts to have a happy marriage, happy family, and happy life. In addition he has been a lifelong student of biology, psychiatry and psychology particularly as they relate to human mating.

The author was married twice as of the writing of this book. The first wife turned out to be an adulteress and despite his best efforts this marriage ended in divorce with irreparable consequences for the children.

The author's second marriage was a casualty of his failure to recognize the numerous red flags, which were present from the beginning of the relationship. He was so anxious to repair his life after the divorce that he failed to take the proper precautions to protect himself from a disturbed, predatory female.

As a result of these failings he was stripped of the fruits of his labor by the divorce industry and an irrational wife. Fortunately, the one thing the lawyers could not take from him was his skill in his profession. His compassion for his patients distinguishes him from those who would destroy him for personal gain. God helps those that help themselves and those who care for the lesser of his children.

As of this writing the author is contemplating a third marriage and a third family this time with proper precautions taken. Truly a triumph of hope over experience.

This book is intended to pass on some of the lessons learned and hopefully prevent the reader from making some of the same mistakes made by the author.

Aaron Burleson M.D.

www.ingramcontent.com/pod-product-compliance
Lightning Source LLC
Chambersburg PA
CBHW060305290526
45789CB00001B/411